Every Cripple a Superhero

CHRISTOPH KELLER

Every Cripple a Superhero

ALLEN LANE
an imprint of
PENGUIN BOOKS

ALLEN LANE

UK | USA | Canada | Ireland | Australia
India | New Zealand | South Africa

Allen Lane is part of the Penguin Random House group of companies
whose addresses can be found at global.penguinrandomhouse.com

First published in Great Britain by Allen Lane 2022
001

Text and photographs copyright © Christoph Keller, 2022

The moral right of the author has been asserted

*This book is a collaboration of languages, English and German. Even though written
in English, it was first published in German. For the German edition the author
worked with translator Florian Vetsch on some parts of the text while he
rewrote others, including 'Bug Story', in German. The editing process was a cross-fertilizing
back-and-forth of the two versions. There are very minor but substantial differences.
In some sense, this is the rare case of a work existing in two originals. CK*

The German version of this book was published by
Limmat Verlag, Zurich, Switzerland, in 2020

Set in 10/13.75pt Warnock Pro
Typeset by Jouve (UK), Milton Keynes
Printed and bound in Great Britain by Clays Ltd, Elcograf S.p.A.

The authorized representative in the EEA is Penguin Random House Ireland,
Morrison Chambers, 32 Nassau Street, Dublin D02 YH68

A CIP catalogue record for this book is available from the British Library

ISBN: 978–0–241–59321–9

www.greenpenguin.co.uk

MIX
Paper from
responsible sources
FSC® C018179
www.fsc.org

Penguin Random House is committed to a
sustainable future for our business, our readers
and our planet. This book is made from Forest
Stewardship Council® certified paper.

Dedicated to my mother

LaGuardia Pl & W 3rd St

I WAS FOURTEEN when I was diagnosed with Spinal Muscular Atrophy. There are three types: SMA I is the most common, the cruellest, the 'baby one' that ends your life in infancy. SMA II, the next-worst, means you'll never walk, spend your life in a wheelchair, likely with breathing support. SMA III, the one I have, I told Jan when we first met, 'is the happiest one': it sets in during puberty, progresses a lot more slowly, and your life expectancy is normal.

SMA is not easy to understand. SMA slows you down. SMA never stops slowing you down. SMA takes muscular functions away. SMA doesn't hurt; its side effects will. SMA is generous, SMA is cruel. SMA is playful; you'll need all your resources to deal with her. SMA is the history of your muscular loss.

Jan wrote about loss in a poem (before we met):

But I say they're singing life,
how we're always losing something,
how beautiful that is.

It is. Oh, it is.

MY FIRST DOCTOR TRIED to explain SMA to me. He said it 'wastes muscles' and that it would put me in a wheelchair by age twenty-five. He was half right: I did acquire my first wheelchair at twenty-five, but I was still able to walk a mile or so, making me a part-time wheelchair user. I kept the chair in the trunk of my car. That way I was equipped for longer excursions. Or for when I was having a bad day. Sometimes I'd walk into a restaurant, sometimes I'd roll. The server who knew me as a walking guest didn't recognize me as a rolling one; and vice versa.

For a few years, there were two of me:

Walking Me. Rolling Me.

Oh, the happiness of SMA Type III.

The doctor, off by ten or so years, in the end, of course, was right.

TODAY I WAS OUT taking pictures of the city's curb cuts. So many have deep cracks or holes, making them dangerous for people wearing high heels, carrying heavy bags, pushing baby carriages, using wheelchairs. A neighbour of ours broke her ankle when she tripped on one. My idea is to send my curb cut pictures to the Dept. of Transportation, shaming them into fixing them. But at home, looking at the pictures, I'm surprised. What I thought would be a crushing visual indictment of New York indifference turns out to be a display of unwitting public art. Filled with water (it has rained overnight) and light (it's a bright early-spring day), reflecting and refracting buildings and people, these ponds and rills have made the hazardous beautiful. They are glimpses of an unacknowledged, mysterious New York; real life collages; portals to another, no less real city. So no, I'm not sending them to the Dept. of Transportation; maybe, when the time is right, I'll send them to the Dept. of Transmutation.

TODAY, I'M ALSO making the reservations for our dear friend Jerry's ninetieth birthday dinner. The restaurant has one high step at the entrance, but they also have a portable ramp they can bring out. We'll be a party of nine. I mention that 'one of us is in a wheelchair'. I don't always say I'm the one. That's my choice.

have you noticed?

people don't say
you're welcome any-
more. they say, No
problem

we used to be
welcome. now
we're not A
problem

Church St & Worth St

THE METAMORPHOSIS is one of the most powerful disability stories ever written. The strength of Gregor Samsa's legs and arms is weakening. Each movement becomes an increasingly enormous expenditure of energy that leaves him more and more spent. Quickly worsening (I am very slowly worsening), he is soon unable to make his way through his room, then even out of his bed (by now I need a lot of help getting out of my bed). At this point, Gregor, who used to support his parents and sister, has become an emotional and financial burden. Wouldn't it be best for his family if he died? Yes, it would; but it's not that easy. How could it be? With Gregor, Kafka is disposing of himself. As so often in his stories, he's trying to undo his own existence. That's why it's so difficult for him to finish them.

I COULD HAVE BEEN diagnosed with SMA a year, if not two years earlier. My two older brothers had already been diagnosed. There'd been plenty of hard-to-miss signs: I couldn't get up from our low living room sofa any more, I had to reach for the banister to climb stairs (and *climbing* it had become), I had to quit my judo classes because what had been big fun only a while ago was now anxiety-producing, a liability, embarrassing. The reason for my late diagnosis was that my family was falling apart. My father's financial recklessness, his spectacular bankruptcy, and his torturous slide into alcoholism were leading to my parents' cruel divorce. Two out of three sons with SMA was enough.

SMA, BY THE WAY, doesn't 'waste' muscles; what it 'wastes' is the connecting currents between brain and muscles. I have a communication disorder. How embarrassing for a writer.

Four-year-old me: kneeling in the sandbox
– rather than crouching like the other kids –
(looking like a Wiener Schnitzel, my mother says).

Six-year-old me: a total wash-out at jump-rope
(that's girlie stuff anyway, my father says).

Ten-year-old me: the slowest runner in school
(but doesn't someone always have to be the slowest runner?
                                        I ask).

MY FATHER GREW UP a plumber's son and was catapulted by the sixties' boom to wealth. He was convinced that rules didn't apply to him and that nothing could stop him. He needed more space for his rapidly expanding metal construction business. Times were glorious. Why just build a factory when you could have a palace, a monument to your work, one with wide hallways that could double as art galleries, one whose offices could compete with the biggest Swiss companies? Keller, Switzerland. The goal was that one day everybody would know what his name stood for. And he wanted more space for his collection. Collections, really. He collected everything. You name it, he collected it. Coins? A pirate's treasure-chest-full. Modern art? Check. African art? Check, and Oceanic art too. Antique toys? Armoires full of them. Armoires? A barn full of them. Church tower clocks? He had so many of them hanging in the attic of our house that the roof threatened to collapse.

DIAGNOSED OR NO DIAGNOSIS, the coach of my high school gym, a staunch believer in pumping iron, decided he could cure what he believed was my 'laziness' with unrelenting exercise. Nevertheless, around that time, a friend started carrying me up the stairs at my stair-infested school: otherwise, with just five minutes between classes, I'd always be late. Next I was exiled from Music: too many stairs for even my strong buddy in this architecturally challenged palace of education (later, however, he carried me down the narrow and very long spiral stairways of the Paris catacombs, 130 steps into the earth to see the bones of the dead, then up 80 at the other end). By the time I was sixteen, the short walk to school had become too hard: I received special permission to drive (in Switzerland the legal driving age is eighteen). It was a used Toyota Corolla, nothing fancy, really just an oversized motorized wheelchair. Stepwise, I just made it to – and through – graduation. If I hadn't – well, I'd have led a very different life.

CAN YOU HELP ME with this bottle, please?

People are not aware that my arms and hands are also weakening. All my voluntary muscles are. It is increasingly harder for me to lift a heavy object (an art book, a flashlight), to open jars, tubes, cans or bottles.

My friend grabs the bottle, drives in the corkscrew and out comes the cork in one swift movement: Ta-da!

Thank you, I say. But did you have to make it look so easy?

IT COULDN'T END WELL. It didn't. The oil crisis of the early seventies was making itself heard ever louder, but my father wasn't listening. The bank that should never have greenlit his vanity factory to start with (as some later stated on record) now dried up the flow of money. It bankrupted my father. It put eighty people out of work. It filled our house with stern-faced men in black suits putting labels on our things and numbers on those labels. The liquidators took paintings from my room – the beautiful collage of a black elephant idling under a green tree by Helen Dahm that I loved so much and still do miss forty-five years later (at heart I'm my father's son in this respect, a collector myself) – they looked under my bed and on top of *my* armoire and went through my drawers, hoping for the legendary stamp collection they'd heard rumours about, instead finding socks, stuffed animals I'd outgrown, pictures of Kate Bush I'd considered too hot to expose to daylight. I could tell they felt sorry for what they had to do to us. If my father had incorporated his company, they wouldn't be here. Why had he insisted on being personally liable? You just didn't do that. You protected your money. You protected your family.

MY MOTHER WOULD HAVE stood by my father through his bankruptcy, but she couldn't endure his drinking any longer. It had turned him into a cursing brute, a lying braggart, borderline violent *and* whiny, ever-filthier, even denying his sons the truth of their disability. Worse, *he* claimed to be the sick one, the victim, the one the world had turned against. It turned my mother into a hausfrau who now also had to be a business woman. She took over the plumbing division that had been a small part of my father's metal construction business. In addition, she became a landlady, turning our single-family home floor by floor into a four-apartment house. Of course, she remained a mother, one who had to take on the role of a father as well.

AND THEN THERE WERE three out of three. We all had SMA, A., born in 1956, M., born in 1958, and C., me, born in 1963. We'd become the SMA-brothers, showing the symptoms of a progressive disability in three stages, I my brothers' image five and seven years in their past, my brothers my own image five and seven years in the future.

Where Broadway Bends

I often sit
in front of Grace Church
at 10th Street,
where Broadway bends.
A cherry tree once stood here,
not giving way,
not even for Broadway.

I often sit
in front of Grace Church,
tourists taking pictures of
no cherry tree
and a man in a wheelchair,
bending Broadway.

> *for Jerry Stern, written*
> *where Broadway bends*

JAN AND I MET DURING the Walking Me and Rolling Me phase. She too thought I was two. This was in September 1997, at an artists' colony in upstate New York. I almost didn't make it there. In May of that year I had broken my ankle, and the head physician of the hospital prescribed a cast. I protested. My muscles would atrophy but, in my case, not recover. A cast would mean the end of Walking Me. He shrugged. Not my problem. I'm in charge of your broken bone, not your muscles. Cast it is, he informed the attending physician and wafted out of the hospital room. Don't worry, the attending physician said once his boss was out of earshot, I'll prescribe orthopaedic boots instead. But you have to promise me to wear them whenever you're on your feet. Wearing those superclunky boots religiously, I was stomping around like Frankenstein's monster. After all, I wanted to recover *and* prove the head physician wrong. I did. It worked. My ankle healed, my muscles didn't atrophy, and September 'found me', as they say in bad biographies, in upstate New York, in a white beauty of a Victorian-style mansion, with a large porch overlooking a vast sculpture garden and fellow writers, translators and artists from all continents walking up and down the hill.

HOW OFTEN DO YOUR FRIENDS *not* invite you to their parties because you can't get in?

Should your friends not tell you about them?

Would you feel better if they did?

Should your friends not organize things you can't attend?

What about your friends' homes?

Should they buy ramps?

Would they reconsider being your friends if they knew that's what they had to do?

Should you choose your friends by whether you can get into their homes?

What if you can get into their apartment, but not into their bathroom?

What if a friend moves from an apartment you can get into to one you can't get into?

Would she or he cease to be your friend?

Should you replace him or her with whoever moved into their place?

What kind of person is friends with you but doesn't make it possible for you to have dinner at her or his place?

Do friends move for a friend?

Who does, if friends don't?

What kind of friend are you to have these thoughts?

I GOT ON THE NERVES of the staff of the artists' colony because, prior to flying over the ocean, I'd kept asking whether what they called their 'handicapped room' was *really* able to accommodate me. Of course, they assured me as many times as I asked them, each time slightly more indignantly. I packed. I made a back-up copy of the novel I planned to work on, *I Like My Country Flat*. I spent nine-hours-plus in the air between Zurich and New York, wondering, Is this the last time I'm flying to America? On the way from Kennedy Airport, I drank a beer on the parking lot of a rest stop out of a brown bag and felt very American. I had dinner with the other residents of the colony, then left the main building, the beautiful white Victorian, as my room wasn't there but in an annex. That didn't matter. What mattered was the step that led to the 'handicapped room'. What mattered was that the door of the 'handicapped room' was too narrow for a wheelchair.

I WAS TOO JETLAGGED to get upset or even consider if that meant I had to leave (and fly back to Switzerland?). Over dinner, we found a solution. The library in the main building on the ground floor would become my bedroom. Even though the upper floors (with the most coveted two guest rooms) and the basement were out of my reach, the ground floor had a comfortable ramp and not a single threshold. They rolled a fairly high contraption, more cot than bed, into what was now my room. The bathroom was within walking distance for Walking Me, the door wide enough and step-free for Rolling Me. By no means, however, would it have qualified as a 'handicapped bathroom'. I was just lucky that my doppelgänger was still around to help me negotiate all that. A few years later it wouldn't have been an option any more. For someone with a different kind of disability, however, it would have been a deal breaker. My boundless gratitude here to the artists' colony for still, in 1997, having no clue what accommodations for people with a disability looked like according to the Americans with Disabilities Act, introduced in 1990. Otherwise, I would not have come. I'd not have met the love of my life.

I reach, I touch, I begin to know you.
(M. R.)

BY THE WAY, it's not called a 'handicapped room'. First, the room is not handicapped, and second, 'handicap' indicates a beggar with a cap in his or her hand. I don't want to be seen like that so don't use that expression.

I ONCE TURNED DOWN the invitation to an art opening, saying, *Thank you, but, from my seated perspective, all I'd see would be asses.* Was that

a) inappropriate?
b) freedom of speech?
c) discriminatory?
d) funny?
e) ungrateful?
f) anti-art?

TALKING TO SOMEONE in a wheelchair when you're standing, do you

a) stay standing?
b) kneel down?
c) say, 'It's so good to see you out and about'?
d) grab a chair and sit down?
e) say 'I'll be right back' and walk away?
f) don't know

IS THE RIGHT TO TELL people what they don't want to hear (to paraphrase Orwell)

a) freedom?
b) obnoxious?
c) sexy?
d) unpatriotic?
e) contagious?
f) a gift?

LET'S GO ON A ROLL, Jan says when she wants us to go on a walk. Walking moves your body and your mind. It's thought-provoking. It's refreshing. So is rolling. Even though all I have to do to move my chair is to steer the 'joystick' of my motorized wheelchair with two fingers of my right hand, rolling is a very physical activity. It's active sitting *and* moving. I have to adjust my balance when I roll up or down a steep street, negotiate damaged curb cuts or potholes, or venture into the woods, provided the paths are good enough and I have enough battery juice. Jan and I fell in love over walk-rolls, and they have deepened our love. A good walk is an intimate, sensual, beautiful affair. We do tree walks, learning the names of trees again and again. We do bird rolls. We do lyric walk-talks. Walks with Eich, translating the German poet. The first poem I translated from the German, albeit not on a walk, was by Günter Eich: *Time for me / to cart off the mountains. / I like my country flat.* Walks with Walser (Robert), rolls with Kafka.

YOU HAVE TO ATTACH THIS to your wheelchair, the ticket sales officer at the ticket office of the enclosed Congo Gorilla Forest in the Bronx Zoo informs me, brandishing a tag displaying the wheelchair symbol. Wouldn't people recognize my wheelchair as a wheelchair without a wheelchair symbol tag attached to it? While attaching the wheelchair symbol tag to my wheelchair, she explains somewhat impatiently that a wheelchair user might get out of his or her wheelchair without warning, thereby creating a danger for other visitors. Therefore, a wheelchair must be identified with a wheelchair symbol tag at all times. Eager to finally see the great apes, I nod and roll quickly down the path leading to the gorillas. Upon leaving Congo Gorilla Forest the tag displaying the wheelchair symbol must be returned to the ticket office, she shouts.

COLLAGE IS THE ART of reconciling contradiction; putting together stray fragments into a coherent new whole is, most agree, the defining art form of the twentieth century. Is *fragmentation* the defining art form of the twenty-first century? In music, it is the technique of organizing fragments into a larger piece of music. In computing, it's storage space used inefficiently. In science, it's a form of asexual reproduction or cloning. In weaponry, it's the shattering of parts and pieces for maximum harm. In life, it's —

If collage is the art of reassembling fragments, then is *fragment-ation* the art of dis/assembling and putting them together anew? This is not the opposite of collage: the original fragments are changed in the process of making and unmaking, then reassembled in a new way. This is not décollage; it's *discollage*. That's what I'm writing: a discollage. Here it is, a life *refragmented*.

THE RESTAURANT WHERE we celebrate Jerry's ninetieth birthday is busy, the space tight. Jan goes inside and asks for the ramp. I'm waiting outside, while other patrons walk up the one step, open the door and go in.

It looks so easy. How do they do it? Lift a leg, take a step, and you're in. I can't imagine any more how I once did it. Once I couldn't imagine what it was like *not* to be able to do it.

In the far corner, they've put a few tables together. Joan and Anne Marie and Jerry, his big birthday smile lighting up the room, are already there. Without asking me where I'd like to sit, our server removes the chair closest to where people must squeeze past to get to the bathroom. I'm larger than the restaurant's chairs, and I've got parts sticking out: handles, knapsack, anti-tippers. I explain this to her. She shrugs. I point at the chair right next to the space where she wants me to sit. She shrugs again. Reluctantly, she pulls away that chair.

Thank you, I say, much too cheerfully, hating myself for trying to bond with her.

We order. We toast Jerry. Once our waitress starts bringing us our dinners, I realize that I've made her job harder. She has to lean over me to put plates down, though it wouldn't have made much of a difference if I sat where she wanted me to sit.

The first two times, she sighs loudly; the third time, she groans into my ear.

Why does he have to sit here? she blurts out the fourth time.

Excuse me, I say, I'm right here.

I wasn't talking to you, she snaps and walks away.

When she returns, I say, Don't treat me as if I'm not sitting here when in every other way you're obviously angry that I am.

I didn't mean it that way, she says, brusquely, unable to hide how annoyed she is with me.

How did you mean it? I ask.

She shrugs and turns away again. It's not her day.

My friends give me a round of applause.

YOU UPGRADE your computer
until it can't take it any more.
You feed your body until
it can't take it any more. Either
way, you'll need a new one.

Become a computer.
(They're working on it.)

Your front wheels attached to
your ankles, your (motorized)
back wheels to your hips, your
battery in your stomach, your
joystick your thoughts.

Become a wheelchair.
(They're working on it.)

Roll me, thoughts, roll me.

A Boy, a Baby, Staring at My Wheels

Rolling down Sullivan Street, full speed,
I notice a boy, maybe seven, watching me.
Staring at me, actually. I know the stare.
He's jealous. My wheelchair moves me so fast,
so effortlessly. *What a cool high-tech tool!*

Rolling further down Sullivan I slow down, passing
a man who pushes a baby stroller, thoughtfully.
The baby is staring at me. I know the stare.
She's scandalized. I'm too big to be in a stroller,
and no one even pushing. *That's baby privilege!*

University Pl & 12th St

AT THE CORNER OF 5th Avenue and West 11th Street I have to stop: there's no ramp at the end of the sidewalk. The curb, however, is not very high. Two inches, maybe less. Can I do it? Or do I have to turn and roll back the entire street block, use the ramp at the corner of West 12th Street, cross 5th Avenue, continue on the other side of the street and cross 5th Avenue again? A long way because of a few inches. I can do it, I tell myself, slowly approach the curb, roll over it and – I badly misjudged.

I land hard. With the small front wheels of my chair in the street while the big back ones are still on the sidewalk, I'm dangerously tilted forward. I'm folding like a jackknife, my chest against my thighs. Reflexively, I stretch out to press against the street. Thus I manage to stop my fall, at least for the time being. But my butt is up, and my head is almost touching the ground. My hair *is* touching the ground. I don't have the strength to push myself back up into the seat; I won't be able to remain in this position for long. The asphalt before my eyes comes closer, starts to blur, simmer.

May I help? I hear a young woman say.

Yes, please, I gasp.

How can I help?

Please, lift my upper body.

She skilfully grabs me from behind and pulls me back into my chair. I'm trembling, but I'm safe.

BUT KAFKA *DOES* FINISH *The Metamorphosis*. That the master of the fragment succeeds in this case is this tragedy's real tragedy. For a long time I thought the ending was the story's flaw. I thought that Kafka, with Gregor out of the way, had lost control of the tone of his tale. Kafka simply isn't a writer of happy endings. To me it didn't *sound* like he meant it. How wrong I was. Of course he meant it – I just didn't want to read it that way. SAMSA HAS SMA! was the headline I heard in my head all those years: I've written about it in my memoir-novel *The Best Dancer*. I realize now that Kafka gave his grisly tale a happy ending, the only one he could conceive of: one without the dung beetle in it. One without *him* in it. Or me. He, Franz Kafka, is The Other, The Cripple, who has come to the conclusion that *he* is the problem. The solution is simple: Gregor must die. Thus, the perfectly bourgeois solution: it's the servant's job to sweep the corpse out of the house. With the dung beetle out of the way (shoved away with a broom!), the remaining family, The Normal Ones, are free, freed again to resume their normal lives and celebrate their normal bodies. The Samsas don't hesitate. As fast as they can, they leave their stuffy apartment behind and travel to the countryside for a life of fresh air. *And they felt it was like a confirmation of their new dreams and good intentions when, as they came to the end of their journey, their daughter was the first to rise from her seat, and she stretched her young body.*

BUG STORY

1

Even though the dermatological irregularity on Dane's body was in a fairly conspicuous spot, it was Jess who discovered it. For Jessica and Dane, Saturday mornings were sleep late, organic drip coffee in bed and reruns of *Chelsea Lately*, followed by love-making. Afterwards (Saturday was also the day Dane changed the sheets), they made the rounds of the health-food stores, then had brunch and more organic drip at the Grey Dog near Union Square. Sometimes they went to Gimme! on Mott, but it was a bit of a walk from their cosy 2BR on West 11th; walking was something they'd rather do on their home treadmill.

As so often on a Saturday morning, Jess was wearing her Happy Roaster T-shirt, part of the coffee gear they'd purchased when they'd discovered Gimme! a few months ago. Dane thought his girl-friend looked – and smelled – darn good in it, fruity, floral, with a fresh blend of crisp citrus and a hint of brown sugar, very much like their favourite fair-trade Colombian. Incidentally, Jessica Moreno's paternal grandparents were from Colombia. On her twenty-first birthday five years ago, she'd changed her birth name from 'Yessica' to the more American 'Jessica'. Now that she was contemplating a career in developing her own line of health and wellness products – bath oils, moisturizers, body washes and hair removal crèmes – changing back to 'Yessica' seemed a smart move. She imagined a large 'Y' as more enticing on the label of her future line.

Usually it was Dane who got the Saturday-morning sex rolling, but this time Jess beat him to it by half a second. She playfully fluted her tongue and wetted his eyebrows with her full lips; she let her tongue slide along the bridge of his somewhat meaty nose. Soon she had 'jumped off' the dimpled cliff of his chin to land safely on his breastbone underneath the coral bed sheets. She patiently worked her way down the familiar territory of Dane's chest, all the while holding his cock firmly in her right hand. Simultaneously, Dane let his fingers wander down the eloquent curvature of Jessica's back. Bubblegum, bubblegum in a dish, how many pieces do you wish, seven, eight, nine? he sang, hopping from vertebra to vertebra. Jessica's backbones each had a Roman numeral tattooed on them. The topless tube of lubricant in his left hand filled the bedroom pleasantly with the fragrance of peppermint. He had already reached vertebra XXI when she said, Dane, what's *this*?

Sitting up quickly, with the sheet wrapped like a scarf around her caffeinated face, she reminded Dane of one of those unsettling fairy-tale creatures, maybe Little Red Riding Hood. From an early age his mother had scared him into obedience with fairytales, mostly German, but also some Russian and Japanese. There was no Danish blood in Dane's family. His first name was both compromise and homage. At the time of Dane's conception Martha and George lived in a railroad apartment so narrow that two people could barely pass each other. They coveted a dog, a great dane, but their apartment wasn't big enough. Martha got pregnant instead.

What's *what*? Dane sat up and looked down his chest.

This! Jess sounded irritated, as though what – whatever it was – was his fault. He couldn't see it, hidden beneath her finger, just to the right of his navel. He always showered that area thoroughly, on Friday nights even finishing up by dabbing his belly button with a Q-tip soaked in witch hazel in preparation for their Saturday-morning lovemaking. Applying the witch hazel made Dane feel pure, hygiene- and relationship-wise. It made Jess happy. She was allergic (in the 'can't-stand-it', not the medical sense) to the somewhat camembert-y odour that collecting sweat and fibre sometimes emit. Jessica was taking a course on the History of Hygiene at the New School for Social Research, while she worked for the Gap on 8th & B'way part-time. The little bottle of witch hazel and the Q-tips had been two of many gifts she'd gotten him for his thirtieth birthday. Other gifts included *Jiro Dreams of Sushi* on Blu-ray and the promise of a five-day trip to Yobal in Colombia, where her grandparents were from.

She removed her finger so he could see what was wrong. It was nothing. He wondered what she could have seen to begin with, in the semi-dark beneath the sheets. Since Jess had taken up meditation again (only a few years ago she had been an 'unbeliever', the way she was now an 'over-believer' – both Dane's expressions), she had started to see things. A saltshaker hovering over the table. Naomi, the six-year-old daughter of the taciturn couple who lived two floors above, floating outside their seventh-floor window, a cute little rascal without wings. Things like that. Dane had considered buying her a popular psychiatrist's new book on hallucinations, but was afraid it might make matters worse. Anyway, it was OK to be in a relationship with someone who had a vivid imagination. He believed it had helped him become more inventive with his cooking, even more fearless, especially with spices. He traced both his inventiveness with, and fear of, food back to his mother's regular reading of fairy-tales. There was so much transformative cooking, so much challenging food in them! There were coma-inducing apples, cabbage that turned you into a monkey! There was porridge that wouldn't stop cooking! Troll toasts, dwarf stew: who knew what that did to you? Soups tended to be beneficial, but there was also that nasty broth the witch was in the process of concocting in Hänsel and Gretel. Dane was convinced that both his mother's fairy-tales and his girlfriend's tendency to hallucinate would some day pay off in his professional life. He simply needed to see the hidden connections.

Look, Jess said.

Dane aimed the bedside lamp down and leaned forward to examine his belly more closely. He could tell now that it was a bit more than nothing; but not much, really. Probably just reddened skin, created by Jessica's finger vigorously applying pressure. A tiny discolouration on which perched a pair of wiry hairs. Both strands pointed to his navel as though they intended to grow in that direction, the way sunflowers grow towards the sun.

Maybe it's a mole, he said.

Did you wash yesterday?

Of course, Dane said. I always do. Especially on Friday nights. He intensified the defensive tone in his voice. Later, when he'd start to bend the impending argument his way, it would come in handy. Didn't he do everything right, and yet so often wasn't she still mad at him? He wondered whether it was something female, something women, and thus men, had to live with. Dane had always been a Johnny-Can-Do-No-Wrong, which could be irritating for a partner less perfect than him. He traced that back to the overly efficient German blood (from his father's side of the family) running through his veins and figured there wasn't much he could do about it. Oddly enough, winning the argument often felt to him like having lost it. That was the drop of Russian in him (from his mother's maternal ancestors).

Dane was convinced that this you-won-but-you-lost thing also had something to do with those merciless fairy-tales: you always found yourself trying to get out of some gingerbread house or wolf's stomach. It was another hidden connection it had taken Dane a long time to see. Now that he did he planned to propose to Jessica, maybe even this spring. May was Jess's favourite month.

She said, Was it already there yesterday? Your mole thing?

I'd have told you.

Have the thing checked first thing Monday morning.

From that moment on they referred to Dane's dermatological inconsistency exclusively as the thing.

Jess said, Let's go to Gimme! today, not The Grey Dog. I feel like real walking.

TO TAKE A SHOWER or a shit, I have to use a polyurethane commode, a chair on wheels with a big hole in the middle. It's a movable toilet that does not use running water. It comes with a container underneath the hole that can be removed to be emptied and cleaned. That's not how I do it. I use it on the actual toilet, without the container. For that I need Jan in the morning to help me from the bed onto the commode and then from the bedroom into the bathroom. Here's how this works. With the help of the remote control of my electric bed I move the bed higher by about five inches: it's a lot easier to get onto the commode when you're higher than the commode. Jan rolls it to my side of the bed and dusts it with baby powder to make sliding easier. She lifts my legs, swings them at an angle of ninety degrees from the bed onto the commode, locks its wheels and, additionally, holds it tight. I press my hands into the mattress, and, using what strength I have in my arms, push and wiggle myself from the bed onto the chair. When I'm all the way on it and we've made sure I'm steady, Jan grabs my legs and swings them again at an angle of ninety degrees to the side so I'm sitting with my back against the back of the chair. Jan unlocks the wheels and pulls me backwards out of the bedroom, through the hallway, then into the bathroom. She makes sure the lid of the toilet is up so I can slide backwards onto it. What I need to do now I can still do without assistance. For how much longer I don't know.

is making
money

writing about
a disability
you don't have

a form of
colonialism?

I hand my
credit card
to the cashier

the cashier takes it
prints out the receipt
and hands both

to you

Broadway
Hey, wheelchair boy!, a Black man shouts, as I'm rolling past him on the sidewalk. Slow down or the mayor will give you a speeding ticket!

West Street
A stretch of the sidewalk is under construction. On the gravel, I skid, I slide, I spit pebbles. It's tricky fun. Handling the joystick of my wheelchair feels like navigating a toy car with a remote control. It reminds me of the boy I once was.

Washington Square North
Die, cripple, die! a white guy yells from the other side of the street.

(A movie theatre. Five people in the audience. The loud whirring of the air conditioner. A spotlight on CK as he rolls in. There's only one spot where he can sit, in the last row, right under the a/c vents. He parks himself there, but realizes that it's chilly and moves down the aisle, where the stream of cold air doesn't hit him. An usher hurries in.)

— This is not where you're supposed to sit. Your seat is in the back.
— It's freezing back there. The a/c blows right at me.
— Here you're a fire hazard.
— There I'll catch cold.
— Move, please. You can't sit here.
— Sir, there are five people in the movie theatre. In an emergency, they'd all be leaving through the *other* aisle because it's much closer to the emergency exit. I'm in no one's way here.
— You *have* to sit in your assigned place.

(CK is tempted to point out the irony to the usher, a Black man, telling him, a man in a wheelchair, where to sit. But he doesn't. Is it possible that the usher has never heard of Rosa Parks who, one day, decided to not *sit in her assigned seat any more, that for 'coloured people'?)*

— I will not sit in 'my' seat. Find one for me where I won't get sick.
— There's nowhere else for you to sit. If you don't go back to your seat, I'll have to call the cops.
— So call the cops. Let me watch the movie until they arrive.

(Usher exits. Lights out. The whirring of the a/cs continues.)

SUPERHEROES! How I love to read about them! They're just packages of disabilities. With supercool prosthetic devices. Superheroes are our Supercripples!

It seems blindness is the most attractive of superafflictions: Dr Mid-Nite, Daredevil, Stick, Madame Web, Blindfold, Hawkeye. Amputees are popular: Misty, Cyborg, Bucky Barnes. Iron Man has a heart condition, Thor a limp. Deafness is rare: Echo. Even rarer is Meniere's Disease, causing extreme vertigo: Count Vertigo, who is also half deaf. There are several paraplegic superheroes: Chief, Oracle, Captain Marvel Jr. Some, like Professor X, are on-and-off paraplegics, which in my book is cheating. You can't turn off a disability. That's the source of your superpower. To live with it, always, in a world that's not made for it. I'm SMA-Man, OK? My superpower is my muscles: the weaker they get, the stronger I become.

What's the one thing that kills a superhero? Not knowing what his or her disability is.

I'M AT THE KNICKERBOCKER Bar & Grill, our neighbourhood steakhouse, known for its jazz and 28 oz. T-Bone (forgive me, vegans!). Celebrities fill both the tables and the wood-panelled walls, many of those on the walls drawn by legendary cartoonist Al Hirschfeld. Leather booths, brass rails, bar. Even the marble bar is legendary: at this bar Charles Lindbergh signed his contract to fly across the Atlantic. Wait, this needs a bit of clarifying. Lindbergh did indeed sign his contract at this marble bar on June 2, 1926, but the bar counter itself was then in a restaurant in Springfield, Illinois. So you see, when you enter the Knickerbocker, you agree to a different kind of journey: you time-travel back to the jazzy, gory glory of old New York, ca. 1920s.

Our friends are ahead of us on their way to our table, unaware that I'm stuck: the row of chairs on my left together with that of bar stools on my right is hard to get past. Jan is behind me. The clinking of glasses, the clattering of silverware, I'm hungry too. The restaurant is crowded, noisy, why did the server lead us through the bar and then disappear? Why didn't the maître d' give us our usual table, near the front – the one that I, by the way, reserved?

I'm not going to ask the people at the bar to move. High up, with their backs towards me, they wouldn't hear. I focus on the four chairs that block my way, one after the other. I ask the occupant of the first chair, an elderly gentleman who might be one of the celebs on the panelled walls: Sir, excuse me, could you please move your chair a bit so I can get through?

The gent is not deep in conversation, he hasn't got his steak yet, but he has already had half of his glass of wine. However, he hesitates. He looks at my wheelchair, then at the space between his own chair and the table.

Coming to the conclusion that this is a reasonable request, he finally says, Of course, and slides his chair towards his table by about an inch.

It's just enough for me to squeeze past.

One chair down, three to go.

Next is a young man in an old-fashioned tweed dinner jacket who has observed my little interaction. I wait but he doesn't budge.

Sir, excuse me, could you please also move your chair a bit so I can get through?

He too hesitates. He too measures the space between his chair and mine, comes to the conclusion that my request is a reasonable one, says, Of course, and performs his one-inch wiggle for me.

Two chairs down, two more to go.

THIS HAPPENS ALL THE TIME. It happens to me and other people in wheelchairs in restaurants, in concert halls, at cocktail receptions, at readings, on sidewalks. People see us but they don't make room. People see how other people just made room for us but still don't move. We have to ask them. Do they not understand what we could possibly want?

Sad lives they all live.

Because we, in wheelchairs, possess a very special kind of power. Fully visible we're invisible. We're right here – and yet we're not. We're not transparent. What is the word I'm looking for? Lucent? Diaphanous? Permeable? No, here it is: We're superinvisible!

UNTIL I WAS THIRTY-TWO OR SO, I could still walk a bit, fifty yards, two hundred, sometimes more, depending on how strong I felt. I walked into a restaurant, sometimes with a cane, or holding someone's arm, or not even that; I walked into a movie theatre; I walked around as much as I could in my apartment. All those years, though, the wheelchair waited for me in the trunk of my car. I chose to get one so early in my career as an SMA-gene carrier because it kept me exploring as much as I still could on my own feet. Because, when I was tired, I could still sit in my wheelchair and explore some more.

I made a similar pre-emptive decision some ten years later. By then the distance I could walk had diminished substantially. I had to be pushed more and more often, too much of a burden for my friends, for Jan, not enough freedom for me. I decided to upgrade from a manual to a power chair; it would get me as far as ten miles, without help. By 'I' I mean we, Jan and me. The power chair was her idea.

I stopped walking altogether when I was forty-five.

TODAY, MY JAZZ BUDDY TERRY and I are going to hear Charles Lloyd in one of the most beautiful settings the musical world has to offer: the Temple of Dendur in the Metropolitan Museum of Art. Millennia-old, Nile-washed sandstone guarantees perfect acoustics for *Wild Man Dance*, the saxophonist's new work, a six-part suite about water and wind. The – *any* – temple is the ideal stage for Lloyd, who makes music a vehicle of utopian peace, cathartic unity, healing prayers, sacred edification. Evocative, poignant, meditative, ever sound-seeking, mystical without getting us too lost, he'll *dream-weave* (to refer to the title of one his best-known tunes) his often very long and protean *soundscapes* (to refer to his idol John Coltrane). Tonight, Lloyd will be playing with the rest of his superb American quartet – Jason Moran on piano, Eric Harland on drums and Joe Sanders on bass – joined by the Greek lyra player Sokratis Sinopoulos and the Hungarian cimbalom player Miklós Lukács.

The main entrance of the Metropolitan Museum on Fifth Avenue is ceremonial, grand, overwhelming. Since it found its headquarters in 1880, the Met has been changed, added to, and altered dozens of times. It was perfectly clear that the only permanent thing about this unique museum would be its unique location: *in* Central Park, where no one, not even billionaires, were allowed to build. They still aren't. Not yet, anyway.

Over the course of the museum's Central Park existence, hordes of architects have added room after room, wing after wing, building after building to the original structure, which was described as resembling a beached whale. It's New York's greatest *improvised* building; for me, it's jazz become stone.

All these riffs and improvisations bring us back to the main entrance. The façade of the building spans four blocks of Fifth Avenue. What's in front of the Met is now basically an overly long, overly corporate plaza, whose recent renovation has cost a whopping $65 million. And it is from here that visitors walk, climb, stroll, waddle or run up the monumental granite staircase – sixty steps! – to enter what might be one of the greatest lobbies of the world, a magnificent echo chamber with its majestic Corinthian arches, its three domes like golden planets above you, its mosaic marble floor under you, its dramatic colonnades, and its countless other promises of the wonders to come, including its large octagonal visitors desk of gleaming marble, where a sea of flowers is always on display thanks to Brooke Astor's generosity. The Great Hall is the welcoming cathedral of the Met: here you pause and take in all the great beauty; here you take a deep breathe before you begin your journey through this miracle of a place.

Yes, here you should begin.

Alas, *should*.

That most accursed of words when you're dealing with a disability, like I do, like millions do. How many times do we hear from people that they are not entirely sure whether a certain place is accessible? Often, that *certain place* is the one where they work, or even live.

Well, they often say, it *should* be accessible.

You bet it should.

I can get into the Met, but I can't do it through the main entrance. Am I asking for too much? But a museum is, above all, about *how* you experience its art. And that begins at the beginning, and that is its main entrance. The aforementioned whopping $65 million was happily dedicated to an unimaginative plaza, a long stretch of paving, punctuated by two lacklustre fountains and a few trees – maybe to remind us that the money for this comes from one of the worst polluters the world has ever known, the Abominable David H. Koch. For this, the beautiful elm trees that lined Fifth Avenue in front of the museum had to be killed. The regal steps, however, were not touched. At least a sign points to the accessible entrance.

Our entrance is a block to the south, at Fifth Avenue and East 81st Street. It is flat, it has automated doors, but ceremonial or grand it is not. On the contrary, it's somewhat hidden away, a practical afterthought. A storage entrance.

First, we roll through a surprisingly windy, dark corridor, then we turn left to have our bags checked by a (usually very upbeat) guard. We roll on, past the Met's fleet of wheelchairs for visitors to our left (the cheap kind we also find in airports, the one a knowing wheelchair user would *never* choose), and to our right past the discount gift shop where discarded items bide their time in the basement until they get carted off.

The Met deprives us of feelings of grandness right at the start of our visit. Given how much money the museum has spent over time for its never-ending expansion, I can't help feeling cheated. Maybe 'discriminated' is the word I'm looking for.

How *else* could it possibly have been done? you might shout. You shout because you think that we should be glad to get in at all. It's a *historical* building! It's *impossible*! It's a landmark not to be *messed* with!

Well, you're wrong. The Met is one of the most messed-with historic buildings in New York. Impossible? In fact these steps were once reconsidered – in favour of a completely step-free entrance. I've seen the 1945 proposal by architects Robert B. O'Connor and Aymar Embury II: instead of the grand stairs they proposed driveways, one from the left, the other from the right side, like in the good old days of the horse and carriage. And it also looks grand, ceremonial! It was championed at the time by Francis Henry Taylor, the museum's director, who was staunchly anti-front steps. They 'strike terror in all persons who reached middle age', he let it be known.

His and the architects' vision was that *everybody* would walk/ roll *barrier-free* into The Greatest Museum in the World through its main entrance, feeling grand. And *everybody* would be ceremoniously welcomed by the Great Hall, feeling even grander. The 1945 proposal is an early and possibly accidental example of Universal Design, aka 'Design That Works for Everybody *and* Looks Great'!

Alas, the proposal was never realized.

What we have instead is steps separating those who can negotiate them from those who can't.

Sometimes a wheelchair feels like a cage,

sometimes a fortress.

11th St & 3rd Ave

TERRY AND I ARRIVE EARLY. We want time to roam, get in the mood. We're going to head to the Met's serene Asian Wing. That's a no-brainer when it comes to Charles Lloyd, the Vedanta master of jazz.

We get our tickets at the admissions desk. I ask for directions to the Asian Wing. I've been here often, but the Met is a maze and you need to know your way around. I know that somewhere on the second floor there are a few steps, but I'm never quite sure how to go around them.

No problem, the admissions clerk says. His directions sound vaguely wrong, but he's so confident and so friendly I don't question him. We dutifully take the elevator to the second floor and turn right. A security guard steps forward and holds up his right hand, traffic-cop-style, almost comically.

Not for you, he says. He points at my wheels. Steps ahead.

At the admissions desk I was told –

Again he holds up his right hand.

Listen to me, he interrupts, imperiously. Take a left, go through European Paintings, turn right into Photography and continue to the Great Hall Balcony. There is an elevator that goes down to the first floor. Turn left and go through the Great Hall and Egyptian Art. Take the elevator on the right back up to the second floor.

The Met is a town – with streets and bridges and squares; a town that unites continents and eras. It's delightful to linger and look; and it's a great place for a rouleur like me – a flâneur on wheels – to roll wheel-loose and map-free wherever the museum takes me. But not today, even though I'm tempted to take a side trip to Gallery 354, the Oceanic Wing with its magical masks, shields, canoes and psychedelic headdresses, maybe my favourite room in New York. Instead, we now have to walk/roll for at least a mile. It takes another ten minutes to get past the enshrined pharaohs and enthralled tourists to the elevator in Egyptian Art. There's a sign on it: CLOSED.

Shouldn't somebody have known about this? Terry wonders.

Should've, I retort.

They're installing something upstairs, the nearest guard I can find says. In Asian, he adds.

That's where we're trying to go. Is the Asian Wing closed?

A part of it, he says.

What about the part that's not closed? How do we get there?

He gives this a thought. Best enquire at Main Information in the Great Hall, he says.

But how come you can't tell us? Terry inquires.

The guard gives this a thought as well. Because I'm in charge of guarding Egyptian Art, not Asian Art, he finally says.

So it's back through Egyptian, back past the astonishingly alive Fayum portrait of a young man and the Mastaba tomb of administrator Perneb, back to the Great Hall. It takes another five minutes. At the elegant cream-coloured beige marble counter of the information desk, Terry does the talking: the counter is too high for a person in a wheelchair. It's also very loud. The Great Hall greets five million visitors a year, and it feels to me that they're all visiting right now. From my seated position, I can't hear the exchange that is going on over my head, but I can watch it as a pantomime. From behind his high stage, the information clerk, doing his best to not acknowledge my existence, alternately looks or points at something in the far distance.

I feel guilty. And left out. Because of me we have to keep asking how to get where we want to go, and now I can't even ask myself. How often has Jan been asked at the airport before boarding, *Can he walk?* And how often did she find herself saying, *Why don't you ask him yourself? He's right here.*

Terry turns, sighs and tells me the guy doesn't really know how best to get to the Asian Wing now that it's partly closed.

It took him a while to say that, I reply. Does he have any suggestions?

To go back to where we started, Terry says, and begin again.

Another ten minutes. This time, the hand-waving guard is gone, but there's someone at the information desk in the corner of the foyer. I roll towards the desk, which is at my height. Unfortunately, the man behind it gets up. Now I have to look up to him, while he talks down to me. Advice to a seated person when a person in a wheelchair approaches: don't stand up.

We've now been in the museum for forty minutes, and we're no closer to the Asian Wing. Far Far East. The man offers three routes. They all sound wrong. I feel strangely patient.

You have no idea what you're talking about, do you? I say serenely, looking up at him.

This prompts a big returning smile – and Route No. 4: elevator back down to the first floor; through Greek and Roman; the Great Hall; left to Medieval Arms & Armour, where, the man announces triumphantly, you will find an elevator that takes you directly to the Asian Wing.

Route 4 works. Finally, we're in Asian. Hooray! What should have taken us a few easy minutes, took us a hard fifty. How far did they make us go, three, four miles? *Put on my tie in a taxi, short of breath, rushing to meditate.* The New York conundrum, as defined by Allen Ginsberg in this 'American Sentence', his version of a haiku. Terry sits down on a bench; I park next to him.

Charles Lloyd, I say, is great.

He is, Terry says, isn't he?

We both look at the colourful eighteenth-century Japanese armour, once worn by a feudal lord of Kishiwada, an artwork composed of so many different elements that it reminds me of a three-dimensional collage, an assemblage, I guess, a hotchpotch masterwork just like the Met itself. We then discover a window from where we can look down on the Temple of Dendur. The chairs and the instruments are already set up. Mysteriously reflecting in the pool in front of it, the temple is reflecting the soothing emptiness of human experience stone by stone. So patient, our temple. Simply endures its fate. Sat once on the holy shores of the Nile, sits now under a glass roof in Babylon-on-Hudson, trampled over by five million tourists per annum. What can you do. Such is life. Totally exists in the moment, the temple. We take a deep breath. We close our eyes. We speed-meditate. We instant-relax. We take the elevator down. We turn left, and there it is –

The back door is ajar. I can see the temple; I can see the chairs set up for the concert; I can even see the long ramp leading to the audience section. *My* ramp. Jan and I have been here before, for a Philip Glass concert. That's when I learned this is the wheelchair users' way in. Fast and easy.

I show the guard our tickets.

This is not an entrance, he says. You have to –

The last time I was allowed to come in through here, I say.

Sorry, he says.

I'm tired, I say, And there's the ramp. I can see it from here. We're so close from the ramp to our seats!

Sorry, he says.

Do you have any idea how many miles we've already rolled through this building to get here?

Sorry, he says.

It is then that an usher appears, opens the door all the way and says, Come with me.

WATER AND WIND. And dance. Music, modal jazz and folk tunes, mystery with clarity, wind and water. Memories of the ancient Nile, early superstar of rivers, now washing us with sound. Lloyd's performing *River*, a swinging BeBop meditation culminating – it is the fourth movement of the suite – in an eddying cimbalom solo. Water, air, stone. The music is taking us to the other world, whether we believe in it or not.

New York City:
Such a beautiful disease
(P. M.)

FLYING, A SOURCE OF ANXIETY for everyone, is an ordeal for us. I'm booking our flights to Switzerland, where Jan and I spend our summers with my family. I wish I could simply roll into a plane, just as I do into a bus. In New York, it goes like this: The bus driver sees me, he signals to the other passengers on the sidewalk to wait and let me board first. The driver pushes a button to electronically unfold a ramp. I roll in. The driver tips up a row of seats to make space for me in my wheelchair. With two hooks on extendable straps the driver secures my wheelchair. Done.

There are no seats you can tip up for a wheelchair on a plane. The only thing reminding you of the existence of wheelchairs is the wheelchair symbol on the bathroom door. The bathroom, however, is not large enough to accommodate a standard wheelchair, much less a motorized one, and a wheelchair symbol on the door doesn't make it any larger.

So the fact is, you *can't* board a plane *in* your wheelchair.

You have to get out of it.

If you can.

If you can't, you're facing a difficult, dangerous and demeaning experience. The airlines require that you be lifted out of your own wheelchair onto what they call an 'aisle chair'. If you've never seen one, think of your own compact carry-on suitcase on rollers, you know, the piece of luggage that just squeezes through the narrow aisles on today's planes. Then imagine installing a metal plate on top of the suitcase, raising the push-pull handle up another 16½ inches. Then take away the suitcase. That's about what an aisle chair is. For any human being, it's an uncomfortable, unsteady, undignified way to travel, even for the shortest distance.

Here's how it works (if all goes well):

You wait in your wheelchair in the boarding bridge just outside the plane. Two flight assistants are on their way. When they arrive with the aisle chair (each time it's a different model, so don't get used to it), they position it next to your wheelchair. They don't greet you, at least not in the US. They also never ask you *how* they can help you. So they don't just grab parts of your wheelchair and limbs of your body, you tell them as fast and articulate as you can what it is you need them to do. Not easy in an anxiety-producing situation such as this. If you're like me, you tell them that you can't hold on to them with your arms if they start to lose their grip. If you don't tell them that fast and clearly enough, there will be an accident. Have your own lines ready. This is when language really counts. Even though the airline is required to let you board *before* everybody else, you're really lucky if this actually happens. What happens instead is that everybody who boards *after* you starts arriving behind you, crowding, eager to get on. What happens now is that everybody is watching you. You, cripple, are holding up the passenger flow. Now you, cripple, have an audience, just like Kafka's ape Rotpeter when he was on tour. So while the passengers are hoping to push past you, the two flight assistants are grabbing you under your arms (from behind) and around your legs (in front of you). Often they struggle, often hard. This is not enviable work. It's hard to get a grip. They're not strong enough (always ask for strong helpers even though it doesn't make a difference). As they're usually men, they do what men do, which is to not look weak before an audience. For you this means it will hurt. How can it not? Someone clutching at your limbs *hurts*. Also in the process your shirt and undershirt are getting pulled up, baring your back and the crack of your ass too. I did tell you this is demeaning, didn't I? And you're not even on the aisle chair yet. For a moment, you're hovering in the air between your beloved, reliable wheelchair and the dreaded, flimsy aisle chair. It's one of those moments that contains multitudes, if I can go Whitman on you.

Your life in the balance. Your body at the mercy (and kindness) of two strangers. At this point you may find yourself raging at the airline executives who refuse to come up with a better system. You'll probably be thinking, if only you could roll into a plane like into a bus! But a plane is not a bus. Right? Wrong! A plane *is* a bus, it is! A bus with wings! A much bigger bus with much more space for wheelchairs. Because flying can be so anxiety-producing, airlines allow on-board emotional support animals, such as: a kangaroo, a snake, a goat, a miniature horse, a squirrel, a monkey, a llama, a duck named Daniel Turducken Stinkerbutt, a pig and a turkey that was rolled through the airport in a wheelchair. But they won't make space for a wheelchair, which is a crippled superhero's legs. *Ka-boom* you land on the yellow-legal-pad-sized platform. Or almost. You'll always be a little bit off. Too far left, too far up front. If too far to the front, you have to act quickly, or else you slide off the aisle chair like a sled down a snowy slope minus the fun. Your helpers will have to adjust your seating position without delay, which involves more grabbing and more exposure of your back etc. If only too far left, you have a bit more time to react, but keep in mind that on a plane every nano-inch is money. The smaller the inch the better. It is conceivable you would think in this moment of despair that the airline bastards have come up with their own measuring unit that automatically shrinks both time and space. A zilch. Yes, a zilch sounds about right. Now hold your breath. Hold your knees (if you can). Keep your hands as close as you can. *You have no zilch to spare.* They tie you down with two sets of belts. Chest first, then legs. Your feet now sit on a rickety platform that doesn't give you the solid support the footrests of your wheelchair do. If you're a movie buff, you can't help thinking of Hannibal Lecter, albeit without the mask. Is that what you are for airlines? A paying cannibalistic serial killer? No time to ponder that. Your helpers swing you around. Now you face your audience. The other passengers have to wait while it's finally your turn to board. Are some of them wondering, Aren't there rules and regulations that ensure that people like this don't hold everything up? Travelling doesn't bring the best out in everyone. You wish you were invisible, while the two guys tip you backwards and push-pull you up the three-inch difference in height between the boarding bridge and the cabin. Not even enough space for a small ramp? You wish you were a less friendly person but you smile back when the flight attendant smilingly welcomes you on board. You wish you were Kafka's hunger artist – why was he complaining about not having an audience? Finally inside the plane, you are turned and squeezed through the corridor that has the exact width of the food cart, past the bathroom with the wheelchair symbol. Your thighs rub against the walls. You're squeezed through business class. You forgive the cranky hag who bangs her carry-on against your knee without acknowledging you. One of your seat belts wraps around an armrest, which annoys the next passenger, so *you* apologize. Your instinct knows better than to rage against business-class-Darwinism. Your helpers back up, free you from the business class armrest, and onwards you journey through the Tunnel of Terror also known as the aisle of the airplane. You've almost made it. This is when one of the helpers asks the flight attendant, *Where does he sit?*, when the flight attendant asks you for your boarding card, and when you point with your chin (your hands are still cramped around your knees) to the scrap of paper visibly sticking out of your shirt pocket. 23B, right there! They roll you next to your seat, unstrap you and try to lift the armrest of the plane seat. But the armrest doesn't lift or otherwise move. Shouldn't the armrest lift? one of the helpers asks. It should, the flight attendant confirms and tries herself. It definitely doesn't lift. Didn't you require a seat with a movable armrest? she asks you. I did, you say, I always do. Behind you, a passenger traffic jam. On a plane, it's always rush hour. Your helpers have to hurry. They don't have the time to consider niceties like movable armrests, requested or not. It seems to you that each time you board a plane they've zilched both space and time even more. And the passengers you're holding up are getting antsy. This is the moment you will dread the most. Again one of the helpers grabs you under your arms, the other under your legs. Now you can feel *their* anxiety. And smell their sweat. This is very hard work, under very wrong conditions. The one who grabs you under your arms has to step behind your seat and its high back to heave you, precisely where there is almost no room to heave; the other one has to lean over to do so. It's excruciating. It's horrible. It's painful. It's demeaning. I know I've already said it, but it is, it really is. Somehow they manage to lift you onto the non-moveable armrest, where you perch for an instant, so your helpers can take a breath and readjust their grip. The one behind you has to reach over the back of the plane seat to pull you up, while the other one shoves your legs along with your butt into the narrow seat with its non-moveable armrest and 11.7 zilch legroom. This, superhero, is where you will be stuck for the next nine hours or so. The superpower that you will now need the most is bladder control. For even if you could somehow get out of your seat, the bathroom is not big enough for you despite its wheelchair symbol. And even if it were, well, you don't have your wheelchair any more.

But I think we need to stop not calling it out. I think that's what we can do. We can stop housing it. So that it stays where it belongs, in the person who's creating it. By not calling it out, it actually arrives somewhere. By calling it out, you're like, you might wanna deal with this, whatever it is for you, y'know? [. . .] people will act defensively, but that's not your concern. I say: You can be defensive if you want. I'm just telling you what I heard and how I feel. If you care about me, then you care about how I feel. If you don't care about me, that's fine. But I'm telling you, it's racist.

(C. R.)

BUG STORY

2

It's *nothing*. Just keep an eye on it.

If it is *nothing*, why should I keep an eye on it?

It's probably not even a mole.

Dane was standing in front of Dr Norris F. Petrossian, with his back against a multi-coloured melanoma chart. He was holding his shirt and undershirt pulled up just high enough so that the doctor could see what he needed to see. Dr Petrossian was a five-foot-four, second-generation Armenian who had treated Dane's family for decades. He liked to crack his knuckles and had a bushy moustache to play with, which helped him make decisions as he diagnosed his patients. Today he was wearing a double-breasted jacket with jetted flap pockets (a style popular in the 1980s) beneath his white doctor's coat. Dr Petrossian himself had a strange hairy dermatological irregularity, which, in his case, sat on his left cheek. Dane wondered whether he'd had it checked out or whether it was true that doctors didn't go to doctors.

So it is *something*? he said.

Of course it's *something*, the doctor said. He had diligently carried on his father's distinctive Armenian accent. It's *nothing* in a manner of speaking. As in *nothing to worry about.*

I'm not worried. My wife wanted me to have it checked out. So now I'm a *little* worried.

Did I know you got married, Dane? Congratulations. George would be so proud of you. You can lower your shirt now.

I'm not, technically. Jess and I are married only in a manner of speaking. Is this *thing* –

Let's not jump to conclusions, the doctor interrupted. So when did you discover it?

It was actually Jess who did when we were . . . , Dane began but fell silent. There was no need to go into their Saturday morning routine. It was unlikely that organic drip-coffee, reruns of *Chelsea Lately* or even lovemaking would shed any medical light on his *thing*. He regretted having referred to Jess as 'his wife,' even if only in a manner of speaking. He already felt that he'd put himself under pressure. This *thing*, he began again, was not on my belly Friday evening, and then, Saturday morning, around ten, it was.

Around ten, the medicine man repeated reverently. What did you do between Friday evening and Saturday morning, Dane?

I slept.

So you see, there's *nothing* to worry about, the doctor said. It'll disappear the way it appeared. It's Mother Nature's oldest sleight of hand. Trust me. Dr Petrossian ascribed everything to nature. A staunch agnostic of the lapsed Catholic sort, he was not ready to believe in God but also not ready to once and for all *not* believe in God. Of course, it can take years to disappear, he said. Nature takes its curse.

His father had said that 'nature takes its curse' was the doctor's favourite pun.

On Saturday the *thing* was the size of a dime. On Sunday it was the size of a quarter, Dane said, and now it's –

Growing in value, Dane.

Dr Petrossian cracked his knuckles, fished out his fob watch from underneath his lab coat and twirled his moustache. The human body grows, and things grow *on* the human body. I agree this can be worrisome, Dane. Dane had his first encounter with Dr Petrossian when he was five. His mother had brought him here with *verruca vulgaris*, or a common wart, on his foot. That too had been nothing, really. Dr Petrossian had recommended leaving it alone, and a few years later it disappeared. Now he said, It is sometimes hard to determine whether it is actually your body growing something, which is usually healthy, or whether it's something living in your body growing something, which can be unhealthy.

The doctor let his watch disappear with a swift movement. Only a small piece of its chain was still visible.

Cancer?

Dane, I do understand your concern. I did everything in my power to help your father, who was more than just a patient to me. He was a dear friend. But what happened to your father has nothing to do with this. And you?

Dr Petrossian scrutinized Dane's somewhat flushed face. Still such java junkies, you guys?

Dane nodded, guiltily.

Not to worry, he said. It can actually be beneficial. Recent studies say that caffeine helps prevent skin cancer. The antidote to too much sun, if you will. You don't frequent those tanning salons, do you?

No, Dane lied.

Good, Dr Petrossian said. Why don't you let me take one last look.

Dane obliged, pulling his shirt up just enough so it permitted a final inspection of the *thing*. This time, Dr Petrossian looked at it through an old-fashioned Armenian-looking magnifying glass that was foggy with fingerprints.

So how's the restaurant business?

He produced a needle that seemed to come out of nowhere and drove it ungently into Dane's belly.

Dane gasped. Then he said, Couldn't be better.

The doctor was poking around inside his belly with his needle.

How come I never see you there, Dr Petrossian?

Pulling the needle out of Dane's body, Dr Petrossian gave him a stern look.

You don't seem to realize how hard it is to get a table at Gulo Gulo. Don't scratch it, he added curtly as Dane let his shirt drop. I'll have the results in a week, said the doctor, looking at something invisible the needle had extracted from Dane's body.

TODAY I'M THINKING OF Mike and John. On 9/11, Mike and John were in the World Trade Center when the planes hit. To make it out of the building alive, they couldn't afford to lose a second. But when they saw a woman in a wheelchair on the sixty-eighth floor, they stopped. Mike and John didn't know the woman. I don't know whether they'd been on the sixty-eighth floor with the woman in the wheelchair or whether they'd been running down the stairs and seen the woman in her wheelchair on the landing. Either way they stopped for her. Others didn't. I don't know whether the other people avoided eye contact or whether they looked at her or whether they whispered *so sorry*, running past her. Maybe they had partners, children to live for. I don't blame them. What are the chances of getting out of that building, hit by a plane and on fire, with no elevators working, when you're on the sixty-eighth floor? Did they even know that a plane had hit the building? But Mike and John stopped. Maybe they were on the same floor and saw her at the window in her wheelchair, watching people falling from higher floors. Were they wondering whether she was considering jumping, preferring that to being burned alive? I don't know. Was that even an option for her? How do you jump out of a window when you're in a wheelchair? I couldn't do it. Maybe they asked her first, 'Can we help you?' and then, 'How can we help you?' Maybe she answered, 'Help me do what, exactly?' Maybe they spotted her from afar and whispered, hurriedly to each other, while still running, 'What do you think, how heavy is she? Can we do it?' Did they say things like, 'Are you out of your mind? It's sixty-eight flights of stairs!' I don't know. Maybe more people ran past that woman in the wheelchair, and Mike and John simply didn't want to live with the memory that they could have done something. Maybe *they*, carrying that woman down sixty-eight flights of stairs, had to run past other people in wheelchairs, waiting for their Mike and John, and how do you live with *that* memory? I don't know, and I don't want to know. Sometimes I just want to think of Mike and John carrying that woman in the wheelchair they didn't even know down sixty-eight flights of stairs out of a building that had been attacked by a plane and was about to collapse.

BUG STORY

3

Dane did his best to ignore the *thing*. He checked it, of course, and quite often – how could he not? – but told himself to listen to the doctor and not worry about it. Why should the patient worry if the doctor didn't? He did, however, cancel his tanning salon session.

Jessica agreed. She also felt better.

Maybe it's just something you ate, she declared.

Later that day Jess saw the six-year-old Naomi from upstairs fly past their living room window. The saltshaker was also briefly hovering over their dining room table. Dane wondered whether she could have hallucinated the *thing*. But each time he checked, it was still there, a sand-coloured island with its pair of hairs sticking out like tiny palm trees on the otherwise pale skin of his belly.

Let's monitor it, Jessica said. Let's be aware of it. But let's not obsess. The important thing is to remain calm.

I am calm, Dane said.

You worrying, Dane, will make things worse. It might actually turn *nothing* into *something*.

Let's talk about something else.

Like Jessica, though in a more limited sense, Dane believed that things constantly said out loud could make things happen, good and bad.

Think positive. That's what we should do.

Jessica lit up like a light bulb. For an instant, she appeared before Dane's mind's eye, meditating, in lotus position (and a sexy pink tanktop), her face flowing like a candle. That's it, Dane thought, looking at her, Jess is more candle than light bulb.

That's it, Dane! she said. From now on we look at the *thing* as something positive. As change. Change is terrifying but also a good thing. Like trying out a new coffee blend.

Or a new coffee shop, Dane said. I've heard good things about The Beanista on St Marks.

Between 2nd and 3rd?

He nodded.

Let's go Saturday.

WE'RE STAYING at our beloved noir-ish motel on Long Island's North Fork. At any time, you expect a grifter, an ageing boxer or at least a PI in his wrinkled trench coat to come out of one the rooms to the soundtrack of the lonely American flag beating the wind. We're likely here for the last time: getting in and out of the bed in this place has become too hard. I can't tell whether I've gotten weaker or whether the hotel has bought a different mattress. What worked for me a year ago – wiggling my way onto my commode – doesn't work any more. I think of all the people who can simply jump out of bed.

I'M WATCHING a guy walking along the beach. He stops and starts throwing stones into the water. Is it possible for a guy to stand by the water and *not* throw stones?

JAN SAYS IT made her happy to sit on that boulder by the water. It also made her sad that I couldn't be with her. That I can't do it. Sit on a boulder by the water, throwing stones. I say I watched her sit on that boulder from our hotel room and it made me happy as well. How many people sit on a boulder by the water like that, I wonder, not really experiencing what they have because they don't know what they could not have?

ON OUR WAY home from the North Fork we passed a burned-down church. All that is intact is a long metallic ramp, leading straight into the black ashes.

(*Dark stage. A spotlight on* MR CHRISTOPH *in a wheelchair, centre stage, a precise circle of light around him.* MR CHRISTOPH *is on the phone. Over loudspeakers:* We thank you for your patience, your call is very important to us. We thank you for your patience, your call is very important to us. We thank you for your patience, your call is very important to us. *A loud click, Marvin Gaye singing 'Mercy, Mercy Me'. After a while, another click, and the music stops.*)

— My name is (*incomprehensible*), how can I help you today?
— Hi, my name is Christoph Keller, how are you? Er, I'm in a wheelchair, and I need to make sure –
— What's your ticket number, Mr Christoph?
— 0162439451855 and 0162439451856. That's my wife's –
— Date of flight?
— June 2, 2015.
— Destination?
— Zurich, Switzerland. From Newark.
— (*after a while*) I can't find your ticket.
— I booked through United.
— Then you'll have to call United.
— I just did. They said my flight is operated by Swiss, and that I have to call you.
— That's correct, Mr Christoph. Your flight is *operated* by Swiss, but United has *issued* your ticket. You have to reissue your ticket and send it to Swiss.
— But I didn't want to fly Swiss. The last time I did, the attendants dropped me. That's why I booked United, three months ago. So I book United, but end up at Swiss anyway?
— That's correct, Mr Christoph.
— Listen, the point is, when I booked with United a lovely person named Lynn . . .

(*Spotlight on* LYNN *who enters the stage, carrying a few cardboard boxes. She drops the boxes.*)

. . . said she gave me the bulkhead seats, my wife and I . . .

(*Spotlight on two very small people, pushing a row of airplane seats on stage. They assemble the cardboard boxes and build a wall, then place the seats in front of them. It takes them a while to get the distance between the cardboard wall and the seats right.*)

LYNN: Voilà: bulkhead seats! With extra legroom! The ones Mr Christoph thought he had reserved! (*Exits, smiling and waving.*)

(*The two very small people put up a curtain next to the bulkheads. On the curtain there's a sign that says,* BUSINESS CLASS: GO AWAY. USE YOUR OWN BATHROOM.)

. . . but she never wrote to confirm that. So I *wrote* to United, asking for these seats *in writing* . . .

(LYNN *crosses the stage again, this time with a yellow legal pad, scribbling something on it.*)

. . . but I never heard back.
— It's absolutely impossible for me to assign seats. That's done at check-in.
— Wait a minute. (*Pulls out a huge book, flips through many pages, comes to one.*) The US Department of Transportation requires that an air carrier assign an appropriate seat to a 'qualified individual with a disability' – that's me. (*Silence*) Are you there?
— Do you need assistance, Mr Christoph?
— I do. I travel in my own wheelchair, and I roll right up to the aircraft. But I'll need an aisle chair . . .

(*LYNN enters pushing an aisle chair. On it sits a modestly obese person with a big sign saying* MR CHRISTOPH. *Several seat belts strap in* MR CHRISTOPH. *He looks miserable. When* LYNN *starts to move the aisle chair,* MR CHRISTOPH *holds on for dear life.*)

. . . and two tall, strong people . . .

(*The two very small people jump up and roll* MR CHRISTOPH *on the aisle chair sideways next to the bulkhead seat. They undo the belts, try to lift him, without success. During the rest of the scene, they keep trying to lift/pull* MR CHRISTOPH *into the chair. After a while they give up and exit.*)

. . . to lift me from my chair onto the aisle chair, roll me down the aisle, and then lift me from the aisle chair onto the plane seat . . .
— How much do you weigh?
— (*hesitates*) About 180 pounds.
— (*clicking in the background*) I have seats for you in row 23.
— Are those bulkhead seats?
— No.
— Do they provide me with more legroom?
— No.
— So what kind of seats are they?
— Regular seats.
— But . . . those don't work for me. I need seats that provide more legroom. I need the extra legroom so the assistants who lift me actually have the *space* to lift me, otherwise . . .
— Those are taken.
— I booked those *three months* ago! So they wouldn't be taken. So if they're taken, they're taken by me. Are you saying someone else has taken them?
— That's correct, Mr Christoph.
— Can I please speak to your supervisor?

— You'll have to call again.
— Why? At what number?
— This number.
— Can't you connect me to a supervisor?
— No, Mr Christoph.
— Although it's the same number?
— Call again and ask for a supervisor.
— I'm asking for one now. What's your name, please?
— My name is (*incomprehensible*). what else can I help you with today?
— No, no . . . I just –
— Please stay on the line to participate in our customer satisfaction survey.

(*A click, followed by a recording of Marvin Gaye singing 'Mercy, Mercy Me'. The two very small people let go of* MR CHRISTOPH *and exit. The actor who has been playing* MR CHRISTOPH *gets up, shrugs, and swiftly walks out. Spot light on* CK. *Slow fade to black.*)

TONIGHT I'M DREAMING I was in our garden in Switzerland, listening to a woodpecker, dreaming of a tower that is all glass and all elevator and no stairs, taking me

> higher and
> higher and
> higher and
> higher and
> *Hello Spaceboy!*
> (*I'm sleepy now*)

He builds his metamorphoses complete and with precision, just like a house. But she suddenly appeared before him as woman in boots, even though she'd just scurried out of the room in slippers.
   (*E. C.*)

Washington Square South & Sullivan St

I USUALLY WAKE UP before Jan. I can reach my tablet on my night table, check the time, my email, the weather, the news. Damn technology, making anxiety so available. I read some Kafka, then something about Max Ernst and alchemy, while listening to Art Tatum over my headphones, all without waking Jan. Blessed technology, making this possible. Before long she wakes up. Rise and shine, my love, did you sleep well? We talk a bit, then I try as best as I can to wiggle myself into 'exercise position'. Until not-so-long-ago I was able to do this on my own: I sleep on my right side, but to exercise I have to lie on my back. Halfway there, I'm waiting for Jan. Recently, she's discovered sheets made of satin weave polyester, making moving in bed easier for me. She grabs me by my left leg and pulls me over until I'm lying flat, as immobile as Gregor Samsa, though he could still wiggle his legs. She lifts and stretches my legs one at a time; the other half of my morning leg exercise I can do myself. I can grab hold of each lower leg, pull it towards me, release it, then do it with the other leg. This feels good: it mimics walking, relaxing my muscles in a way I can't do any more; it eases the feeling of heaviness that night inflicts on my muscles. I reach for the remote for my adjustable bed and press a button. The back of the bed rises until I'm sitting up, or almost: Jan, at my side now, is gently pushing me forward the rest of the way. This last push is another thing I didn't need not so long ago. While I lower the back of the bed, then wiggle back – sitting up with the help of an electric bed has the side effect of sliding you too far down on your bed – Jan's bringing the coffee, the newspaper. It's nice to do this in bed, together, with no rush. We also have breakfast here; for me it's my 'keep-my-weight-at-bay' drink, powdered vitamins and minerals in low-fat milk. This also gets my metabolism started: bathroom time! Jan brings the shower commode, and once we've got me onto it (for full procedure see p. 38) she rolls me into the bathroom and, backwards, onto the toilet. When I'm done, I call her, and Jan rolls me back to the bed. She lifts my legs onto the mattress, rolls the commode up close to the side of it and locks the wheels. She pulls me into the bed legs first, then hands me my clothes. I put on my undershirt, my shirt, my socks. Underpants and pants I can pull almost all the way up. Then I need her help again. I roll on my belly, she wiggles my pants up; I roll on my back, she helps me zip and button my pants. She grabs my legs and pulls me to the edge of the bed, until my feet touch the ground; until I'm in sitting position. She helps me with my shoes; parks my chair sideways next to the bed; puts the transfer board, a banana-shaped (and banana-coloured) piece of plastic half under me, half onto the seat of my wheelchair. I wiggle across it, inch by inch, slowly, with the help of my arms, into my chair. Together we install the footrests, together we lift my feet onto them, and I switch on the power of my wheelchair.

This is when I hear the sound of one hand clapping.

KAFKA SUFFERED FROM digestive problems, debilitating head-aches, insomnia; from shortness of breath, rheumatoid backache, rashes; from noise oversensitivity, exhaustion, terror of commit-ment; from his big ears and his deformed toe; from his father; from panic attacks; from fear of losing his hair and his eyesight. It sent him from one spa to the next, made him a veggie, a nuteater, a Fletcherian, a fitness freak, a marriage seeker. Was Kafka disabled? Hard to say. He must have felt that there was something in the world that disabled him or he would not have written what he wrote, over and over again, attempt after attempt about people in a world that disables them, usually for no reason, just because it can.

WHEN WE'RE IN ST GALLEN in the summers, we're at my mother's house. This is where I grew up, in a stately four-storey house that my family once – in statelier times – occupied in its entirety. But for more than three decades our house has been divided into four apartments: my mother's apartment, two rentals above, and Jan's and mine beneath. It is a remodelled basement; we prefer to call it our garden apartment. Since the house is on a slope, we have windows with lovely views on three sides. Ironically, I can't enter my childhood home through the front door; but I have two other options: through a side door that leads to the foyer and, with the help of a stairlift, down the eight steps to our apartment; or down a short path running alongside the house to our bedroom that has a door to the garden. That's the way I prefer: it means I don't have to operate any more machines than the one I'm already sitting in.

Our apartment has an abundance of charm. When I was a child – when my family were the sole occupants of the house – it hosted our *Tobzelle* (literally a 'padded cell': our expression for our playroom gone wild), and what we called *Beiz* (the cellar – or *Keller* – a version of a downstairs dining room complete with an old restaurant table and a huge fireplace), where we had small parties, as well as our wine vault, which my father frequented a bit too often. The floors are old terracotta, grainy in texture and with lots of stains, each stain telling a microchapter of my youth. The doors were marvellous, carved wooden ones my father rescued from demolished houses; one is even integrated into the wooden ceiling of our kitchen, making you wonder what would happen if you'd open it. There's an old sandstone column (for show, not support, but who really knows at this point?), a fireplace, painted chests and armoires, the latter once the pride of local farmers who had these precious and beautiful things made for their daughters on the occasion of their weddings. Names like Annelis and Karl Sturzenegger and Babette and Otto Zuberbühler, painted above the doors of the armoires – names of people we've never met or even know anything about – live with us, watching over us.

We feel safe here; here we're happy.

The low ceilings make for additional *Gemütlichkeit* (cosiness) unless you're really tall. But low ceilings are not an issue when you're in a wheelchair. The apartment is our roll-in cave, and we decorated it with cave art: prints and paintings and pitchers and other things we find in the flea markets we both love to roam.

They're so proud of him:
He never complains!

He keeps telling them:
You're not listening!

TODAY WE'RE IN HERISAU, a small town about ten kilometres west from St Gallen. It's a pretty but rundown town, abandoned by the rich to the workers. If this were New York, eventually the kind of people who hypergentrified the meatpacking district into 'The Meatpacking District' would get around to it. For the time being, it's still the town where Robert Walser spent the last twenty-five years of his life in the psychiatric hospital: *I'm not here to write, but to be mad.*

A narrow path, wide enough for a wheelchair and not too steep, leads off a path of the small rose park we've discovered down to the gate of the back of a restaurant. We have dinner in the garden of the workers' restaurant. We have to be finished by 8 p.m. as that's when the park closes. There are steps into the restaurant so the park is my only option. What if we'd miss our curfew? How would we get out? Find the person who has the key to the rose garden? But we don't worry: it's too pleasant. *I'm not here to be mad, but to have dinner.*

The way the paths looked in the evening light, it was clear they were paths home.
    (R. W.)

TODAY I'M SEEING my doctor at the SMA Clinic in St Gallen for my annual check-up.

'You've lost weight,' he says.

Since it's laborious to weigh me (it involves a hoist), we agree that I lost 4–5 kg. Last year we estimated my weight at 99.9 kg (219.8 lb); now we settle on 95.7 (211 lb). I promise him to lose another 5 kg (11 lb) by the next time I see him. Keeping the weight at bay is the most efficient way to keep SMA at bay: the less you weigh, the less your muscles have to lift. Simple as that. Gravity.

'What has changed since last year?'

'The airline seats,' I say. 'They've gotten even smaller.'

The doctor laughs. 'Don't you fly business?'

'Who can afford that?' I say. 'I read that Swiss Airline has plans to introduce their new "innovative seats".'

'What's innovative about them?'

'Once you've successfully squeezed yourself into them, they'll automatically minimize your size.'

He laughs again. 'What else?'

'I'm more or less as I was a year ago. It's become harder for me to wiggle around or turn over in bed.' I tell him about the sheets Jan has found. They help.

He nods, makes a note.

I imagine him writing, *Every person with a disability is a superhero.*

'At night, I sometimes have a numb pain in my right leg,' I say. 'Never during the day. It could be sciatica,' I self-diagnose.

The doctor asks me a few more questions. I might be right, he says. There are pills that could ease the pain, there's surgery.

I ask, as I ask every year, 'Still no miracle cure?'

'Still no miracle cure,' he says, as he does every year.

If all else fails, the cripples will resort to violence with their crutches.
  (J. F.)

THE HORROR OF Gregor Samsa's metamorphosis is that he didn't change inside. He still thinks like Gregor Samsa, knowing that he's woken up in the body of a dung beetle, knowing that he's a travelling salesman who has parents and a sister who rely on him. He also knows that he has missed his appointment.

How much easier would it have been to wake up as a dung beetle who also thinks dung beetle thoughts! No more wondering whether this was a dream. No more paying attention to the lady in a fur hat and fur boa in its pretty gilt frame on the wall. His ambition, if that's the right word, would have been to feed. He would not have found much to his liking in the Samsa apartment so: the parents and the sister would have been relatively safe, I assume. He would have found a way into the street, probably out of Prague, following his instinct until he'd found a forest or grasslands that better suited his being a giant dung beetle.

That, of course, is an entirely different story.

The true horror of being disabled is knowing that you're disabled and knowing that the world perceives you as such.

As a monster, as a dung beetle, a deformity, a disgrace, a sorrow to your family, a waste of money, not a money maker any more, an obstacle in every respect.

How do you live with *that*?

That is what Kafka dares to ask in *The Metamorphosis*, bravest, cruellest of all tales.

Cripple outside, superhero inside.

BUG STORY

4

On Wednesday Dane asked Lofty Liu (whose actual name was Leonard L. Lewis), Gulo Gulo's manager, for a favour. Could Lofty please call Dr Norris F. Petrossian and offer him a table? Despite his name, Lofty Liu was a handsome androgynous little shit of Sicilian-Chinese descent with thick black eyebrows on the verge of growing together and a birthmark the shape of Sicily and the size of the Sichuan province on his forehead.

Anytime except Fridays or Saturdays, Lofty said with a triumphant but sad look in his eyes. Those days were booked solid a year in advance.

Lofty was longing to change the restaurant's reservation policy so tables could not be booked more than four weeks in advance. That was how most upscale New York establishments handled things on this long and narrow island so densely populated with foodies. Some joints had even stopped taking reservations altogether – but, despite his relative youth and insider access to hipster fooddom, Lofty was old-school. He believed knowing in advance that you had a table in a restaurant was part of a pleasant dining experience. He couldn't for the life of him understand why freezing your ass off for hours on a cracked sidewalk was considered so hip. Dane hadn't formed a definitive opinion on the reservation subject yet. There were as many pros and cons as there were variations on skatefish à la beurre.

Satisfied with Lofty's answer, Dane went about his work as the restaurant's emerging second antipasto chef and almost completely forgot about the *thing*. He had already gained a loyal following in the food universe with his antipasto-portioned troccoli all'arrabbiata al Dane. The pepper unfolded its taste unexpectedly gently on the diner's tongue until his or her guard was down; then it unleashed its arrabiata unrestrained. The troccoli dish was best served with a crisp Tocai Friulano (and a large earthenware pitcher of New York's fabled tap water). This inspired choice was a collaboration between Dane and the Gulo's chief sommelier. Then Dane wowed the gourmet world with his spa-ghetti neri frutti di mare piccolo. Again it was a textbook example of understated cooking, subverting the prejudiced notion of an acquired taste. With the 'neri', as Dane referred to his creation, it was the pedestrian tomato-based sauce whose image he spruced up with the unorthodox use of Ghost chillis, or Bhut Jolokia, peppers twice as hot as the hottest habaneros, that, chopped the right way, arrived on the taste buds with just the right bite. Tangy but not rabidly so. All'arrabbiata ma non troppo.

Jessica didn't have the luxury of being distracted by serious work. With a little more time on her hands than was good for her (in Dane's opinion), she was doing exactly what she'd said they shouldn't do and obsessing about the *thing*. She had developed an aching fondness for it and started to think of it as more hers than his. It was often like that with her, one extreme feeling invit-ing its opposite, repulsion becoming ardour – often overnight – and always without warning. Dane remembered only too well how she'd transitioned from despising children (especially six-year-old Naomi from upstairs) to fantasizing about having a bunch of her own. Now she played with the ever-more-numerous strands of hair growing out of the *thing*. She even kissed it, while kissing the rest of Dane a lot less. On Wednesday night she waited until Dane was asleep so she could crawl under the sheet and play with the *thing*. Jessica told him that she felt protective of it, a solid, warming feeling she hadn't experienced before in her life.

BY RUBBING THE PATTERN of a plank of wood, a piece of torn cloth or a leaf onto paper (*frottage*), Max Ernst avoided 'authorship' of his works.

Kafka did something similar, stripping his German of all its Bohemian/Prague/local origins to its bare bones, thus creating the almost authorless, universal and inimitable Kafkadeutsch.

It's a kind of Frottagedeutsch, achieved by rubbing the pattern of language onto paper.

TODAY WE'RE GOING to send our letter again to the president of PEN, the writers' organization fighting for freedom of expression, for the freedom to write. Jan and I haven't renewed our membership in protest at PEN hosting events in venues that are not accessible – that means we're not free to hear, doesn't it? We keep sending the letter until we get a reply.

RBF – Resting Bitch Face – is the latest in misogyny. It's the woman's version of 'bitter': smile, don't be a bitch.

Be bitter.
Be a bitch.

ConEd Poem

Smell rotten eggs?
Suspect a gas leak?
Act fast. DO NOT use a phone,
DO NOT light a match,
DO NOT turn on or off:
lights,
flashlights,
appliances,
or any device that could create a spark
and cause the gas to explode.

What do you mean, dear ConEd?
Should I NOT turn on
or off my wheelchair?
Should I NOT roll out of the apartment, down
the hallway to the
elevators, where it says,
IN CASE OF FIRE USE
STAIRS?

5

By Thursday morning the *thing* was approximately the size of a soup ladle (without the handle). It had darkened a bit, at least at its centre, while its banks, if you wanted to call them that, had preserved their sandy colour. At 4 p.m., just before changing into his chef scrubs, Dane checked it again. If it weren't for Jessica calling to see how the *thing* was doing, and one time even calling it 'her' *thing*, he would have forgotten about it during his typically hectic shift. But instead, Dane cooked with the *thing* on his mind. An unusual number of antipasti, including three neri, were returned untouched or even vivisected (as though the guests had been digging for the secret of its taste). These heartbreaking journeys back into the kitchen were equalled in number by appearances from Lofty Liu. Lofty was a good guy, but when he saw the opportunity to humiliate someone in front of others he didn't think twice. That evening the entire kitchen staff had a good time at Dane's expense. Lofty, who had a crush on Jessica, confiscated Dane's phone so she couldn't distract him any longer. Fewer antipasti came back; it was a rotten evening all the same. At the end of his shift, Dane checked again. It seemed to him that the *thing* had stopped growing. But he was too exhausted and too disappointed to decide whether that was a good thing or not.

Drifting home through the dark and contorted Village streets, the depressing smell of untouched antipasti still in his nose, Dane pondered his fate, determined not to let the *thing* (or any other thing) get in the way of his generally good fortune. Gulo Gulo was one of five restaurants in town (all below 14th Street, where the real City was) owned by LMC, rap-star-turned-celebrity-restaurant-owner. They were all hugely successful, farm-to-table eateries, specializing in chic comfort food with an Italian accent.

Though Dane had never met LMC in person and didn't even know what those letters stood for, he considered LMC his capital-M Mentor; even if he didn't exist or was really no more than three letters, it was clear to Dane that he, Dane, owed his existence in the restaurant world to LMC. It was in the kitchen of Gulo Gulo that the pendulum of his life had swung from prep cook to antipasto chef; it was here, in the presence of the gilt-framed Basquiat-style portrait of LMC (copies of which hung in all of his kitchens), where Dane, peeling garlic and dicing onions, had first had the inspiration for his best food inventions, the neri among them. One day, thanks to LMC, he'd either have his own celebrity restaurant or be the executive chef of one of LMC's joints. But, essentially risk-averse, Dane had no desire to be his own boss. Being a star chef in the kitchen, not a crackerjack at the helm of some shiny business empire, had been his declared goal ever since he started at Gulo Gulo three years ago. By now Dane considered his ascent in the gourmet world inevitable.

The worst that could happen was that he got sharked from LMC, by Tamabili maybe. He wasn't eager to work for Rio Tamabili, not even hypothetically. He didn't think that an offensive dresser like Tamabili – with a wardrobe that seemed limited to frayed polos, cut-off sweatpants and cheap flip-flops – should be successful in a business that required delicate refinement. It was almost as though Tamabili meant to insult the gourmands that flocked to his restaurants. Was it possible that all these people spent astronomical amounts of money for, admittedly, divine food *in order* to be insulted?

Jess, who was eager to be her own boss one day, called Dane's lack of interest in either his own restaurant empire or a high-profile job with the highest profile restaurateur in NYC 'unambitious'. Dane called it 'realistic' and 'focused', both characteristics he didn't associate with Jessica's approach to her future. He couldn't for the life of him fathom how working part-time at the Gap, inattentively practising meditation, and studying the washing habits (or absence thereof) of ancient people could possibly add up to anything substantial. He considered Jess's plans for her own line of personal-hygiene products at best an ambitious hallucination.

As he approached 11th Street, Dane felt a tingling in his *thing*, not unlike the tingling he felt when Jess licked his skin. It was a feeling that came from deep inside his body, something comforting and arousing that assured him that he was not alone on this planet.

On Friday it became clear that the *thing* wasn't growing any more; but equally clear was that it was still changing. The area of skin it occupied now surrounded his navel entirely, somehow reminding him of a landing field with his belly-button potentially swallowing up whatever might consider alighting there. It wasn't dark any more, but pink, as in 'baby skin pink'. Unlike baby skin, though, it had hardened to the point that he felt it could crack, like old wood or really dried-out cardboard, if he pressed it too hard. But like baby skin it emitted a soft, fresh amniotic odour, which he believed his body now produced, even though Jess insisted the fragrance simply came from the baby oil she'd asked him to add to the witch-lotion in his navel-cleaning ritual.

TODAY WE'RE ON TOP of a mountain. All sorts of contraptions got us here: a car, elevators, a cog railroad, a skylift. The brand new building is state-of-the-art, architecture-magazine-ready. The star architects did a super job, unless, say, you're in a wheelchair and you'd want to get out of the mountain masterpiece and explore the mountain top like everybody else. All along the length of the building there are rows of steps. This is the face of the building; everybody gathers down there, taking in the view. So much room for a ramp but no ramp. How weird this feels, on top of a mountain, stuck at the top of a stairway. We're here, everybody else is down there, sitting on the steps, walking along the paths, in the grass, in the rocks, among the wildflowers. No ramp at all? Really, can this be? Jan and I go to look for one, finally finding in a remote corner of the building something that might do. But it's safe to assume the star architects had nothing to do with it: just a bunch of wooden planks, thrown together after the design magazines were done praising the new building. This ramp is an afterthought for people who are afterthoughts. It's also too steep. With Jan holding onto the back of the wheelchair, I'm precariously rolling down and onto the gravel path. Gravel and wheels don't play well together so I roll in the grass beside it. We discover that a small fraction of the mountain paths works for anyone in a wheelchair. And the benches don't. They are heavy, clunky chunks of whatever with no space beside them for a wheelchair. So here we sit, Jan on the bench, me in my wheelchair, taking in the mountain view, a garbage container between us.

2nd Ave & 11th St

AND YET, THE YOUNGEST reader may be shocked to consider that, until quite recently, most black literature remained unpublished. This neglect was hardly accidental. Literature, the crafting of language by special, human experience, acts as witness. Great literature acts as an unforgettable, completely convincing witness. Poetry raises the human voice from the flat, familiar symbols on a paper page. Great poetry compels an answering; the raised voice creates communion. Until recently, the Afro-American witness suffered an alien censorship.

June Jordan wrote this in 1970, in her introduction to *soulscript*, an anthology of African American poetry. This also applies to the 'disabled' poet/writer: the witness of the disabled life also suffers an alien censorship. The only examples of disabled writers you can name, if you *can* name any, are the exceptions, the pardoned turkey. We're still more written *about*; our voices are now more often recorded; but are they heard directly?

Disability is mostly managed by the able-bodied. They are our zookeepers, we are their animals. They write books about us and the cages we live in. They write about us to advance their careers. They're our anthropologists, writing their secondary texts about us. It doesn't advance *their* careers when *we* write the primary ones. Writing about us gets *them* grants, prizes, tenure, book contracts, speaking engagements, invitations to conferences and book festivals, seats on boards of institutions that manage the disabled and whatnot. Depriving us of writing our texts takes away all that from us. In addition, it makes sure that the blame for being disabled sits squarely with us.

Much 'disabled' literature still remains unpublished, even unwritten as, more often than not, conditions are too hard for many of us to get through the day *and* get some writing done. Yet being in a wheelchair, being sedentary, *is* the ultimate writing position (never mind Goethe etc. who wrote standing up). Well, maybe – again – the writing can be done, but what about the networking? The selling-yourself part? The being-at-every-event-that-might-get-you-the-attention-of-the-big-shot-reviewer? We simply don't have the energy for that. There are still simply too many obstacles for that (the Swiss trains are *still* not reliably accessible! There's only *one* person with a disability in the Swiss Congress!).

Our alien censorship is also the steps / the distances / the plane rides / the hotel rooms / the inaccessible readings / book celebrations / panel discussions / writers' conferences / the zoo-keepers / etc.

THESE DAYS it is mandatory for your book to have A Concept. So here's my Concept. I'm the Concept.

Concept/Schmoncept

five definitions
in non-alphabetical order

cripple
code for 'disabled'

freak
you thinking you're normal

normal
every freak

disabled
just live long enough
also, code for 'cripple'

superhero
every cripple
(and freak)

BUG STORY

6

On Saturday morning, Dane was preparing a new Guaya'b they'd discovered at Gimme! the week before. The coffee, produced by a cooperative of Mayan-Popti farmers in the Guatemalan highlands, filled the apartment with its rich, musky aroma. According to the company, the beans were grown under lush shade canopies that provided a natural habitat for indigenous as well as migratory birds, earning the brew the distinction of being Smithsonian Bird Friendly®. Jess, scrolling through the *Chelsea Lately* homepage, was choosing a re-run for them to stream in bed. She was wearing her oversized Happy Roaster T-shirt as a nightie; it had started to unravel around the collar but she wasn't ready to part with it. Fortuitously, she came upon an episode in which Chelsea's guest was none other than Kevin Cuddeback, CEO of Gimme!.

Look what I found, Jess triumphantly announced as Dane returned to the bedroom, preceded by the comforting yet subtly arousing scent of Guaya'b. The thought of sex crossed her mind, but it was just that, a thought. She knew she was sexy but didn't feel sexy enough to act on it.

Do you think Chelsea always sits sideways because having such long legs is uncomfortable?

She was waiting for the coffee to cool.

At least that's how I imagine it would be, said Jessica, who measured a mere 4′ 11″, legs included.

Conceivable, Dane said.

He was in a good mood. The coffee was great, and the *thing*, which he had checked in the kitchen, looked smaller, rounder and an even healthier pink than the day before. As far as his unusually long legs were concerned – at least as long as Chelsea's, if not longer – he'd never experienced any discomfort. Neither sitting nor walking, and he had no back problems either. Dane didn't mind at all that he was almost twice Jess's size. However, it was something Jessica didn't like him pointing out, not even jokingly. She prided herself on being self-ironic but drew the line when it came to anything to do with her height.

I *know* what Chelsea's doing.

Jess talked over Kevin Cuddeback, who was saying that if his coffee were prepared properly you could actually sense its fair-trade quality on your taste buds.

Look, she said. Chelsea is exposing her legs length-wise to the camera to make them look even longer.

Even her chair is kind of longish, Dane said. Perspective, you know. Who knows what kind of lens they use. A leg-elongating lens, maybe?

Ha-ha. I'm certain Chelsea's fishnets are responsible for her 72.3 per cent male viewers in the 18-to-34 age group. Is that why you watch, Dane?

I'm watching because you're watching, Jess. Sometimes I'm watching *your* legs while you're watching Chelsea's legs.

That's a sweet thing to say, Dane. She kissed him. What do you think about when you're watching my legs during *Chelsea Lately*?

About steamy post-*Chelsea Lately* lovemaking, he said with a sweet grin.

She kissed him again, reached under the bed sheets and gave his summoned cock a jovial squeeze.

So what do you think of the Guaya'b?

Now that the coffee was cool enough she sipped a bit, put on her Java connoisseur face, gazed at the ceiling for a moment and said, It leaves a bit of a bitter taste, I think.

That's the fair trade, Dane said.

For a while they watched *Chelsea Lately* in silence. Jess had read somewhere that it was not unusual for a girl of Latin American stock growing up in the New York suburbs to have short legs. When it came to attracting the male gaze, however, she'd never had any problems, easily outdoing Chelsea's puny 72.3 per cent on any sidewalk, especially when in a skirt and heels.

Fishnets make me look fat, don't you think?

Nothing makes you look fat.

Dane's answer painted an encouraging smile on his girlfriend's face. As the show's credits started to roll, he turned off the TV, set down his coffee mug on the bedside table and leaned over to kiss her. He was already humming Bubblegum, bubblegum with his fingers exploring vertebra #5, deliciously hidden under her blue Happy Roaster T-shirt, his cock paying homage to her beauty, when Jessica abruptly pulled away from him, wriggling his arm out from under her shirt.

What are you doing? It's Saturday morning!

She adjusted her T-shirt. It's just – she began, looked down and continued, Let's maybe wait till we know exactly what happens next with your *thing*.

It's not contagious or anything, he said, more confused than irritated. Anyway, don't think I don't know that you're kissing my *thing* when I'm sleeping. When she said nothing, he added, in a conciliatory tone, I love it. It gives me sweet dreams. He was as hard as a lug wrench.

Well, then, let me see, Jess said.

She sounded like a concerned mother about to inspect her child's booboo, not a lover about to unleash her diminutive beauty onto her boy toy. His cock presented her with a catch-22: on the one hand she had to shove it aside to see the *thing* while, on the other hand, her holding Dane's cock even perfunctorily made it even harder, obfuscating the *thing* even more.

Whoa!

What? Dane quickly sat up, and saw what she meant. Whoa!

Something creamy-brown, shiny and a bit translucent was poking its head (if that's what it was) out of his navel, beginning a journey on his belly. Dane quickly picked up the small moving object between his index finger and his thumb and crushed it.

Why did you do that, Dane? Jess avoided looking at him.

What do you mean?

Why did you kill it?

I don't know what it is.

It came *out* of you.

He inspected the creature between his fingers.

It's an ant. With wings, I think, he said and flicked it across the room towards the door. If it reached the door, they didn't see it; if it made a noise hitting the floor, they didn't hear that.

What would you have done with an insect crawling around on your body, Jess?

I'd have watched it. She had tears in her eyes. Aren't you curious what the little thing would have done?

It was an ant, Jess!

It was in your belly!

Exactly. *My* belly.

We're in a relationship, Dane, Jess said. Don't you understand?

I'm sorry, he said, not sure whether he did understand. He tried to kiss her tears away but Jess withdrew.

You know, when I look at the *thing* at night when you're asleep, when I lick it I feel – felt something inside it. Something alive. A pulse. A heartbeat. Her voice trembled. If we all killed what comes out of our bodies, humankind wouldn't exist.

But not everything coming out of us is worth –

The phone interrupted him. Worth what? Dane wasn't sure.

Out of Area, he said, glancing at the display of the phone sitting on the night table on Jess's side of the bed. Telemarketing. Don't pick it up.

Jess did anyway. Oh. Hi. Hello, she said and left the room.

He grabbed his book from his bedside table. It was an anthology of recipes for literary characters. Last time, he'd studied the 'Franny and Zooey' cheeseburger; now he checked out 'Apple Pie for Gregor Samsa'.

Who was that? Dane asked when Jess came back.

Norris.

Dr Petrossian?

Jess nodded. She was the only one who referred to Dane's family dermatologist by his first name. Maybe because she still wasn't legally a part of the family.

Letting us know that the biopsy report had just come in by Special Weekend Express Overnight Delivery, FedEx or UPS, I forgot which, something that Norris does only for the Kohler family. And that he was right. That it's *nothing to worry* about.

Dane stared at his *thing* as though Dr Petrossian was about to crawl out of it.

I don't think he's supposed to talk to you about my *thing*, Dane said. Legally. Without my consent. Not until we're married. And even then I'm not sure.

Norris just said it's *nothing to worry about*, she said. It must be legally OK to say that. He also said he wishes you a joyful, relaxing weekend with your future wife. And he said that he appreciated the invitation from Gulo. That was very considerate of you, Dane.

It wasn't a comp. He'll still have to pay. But I'm glad Lofty came through.

I think Lofty has a thing for me, Jess said. And what's the deal with the future wife? Anything I should know?

Dane blushed. Do you mind –

Mind what? Marrying you?

If we don't go to the Beanista?

No, I don't, Jess said. Let's stay home.

After Reading about Max Ernst and Alchemy

I dream of department stores that carry
love potions,
phoenixes,
putrifactions,
petrifications,

preoccupations,
perturbations,
personifications,
purgatories,
planets,
plants
priests,
points,
Prussians,
Philippics,
penchants,
pockets,
plagues,
praise, ap-
pearances, op-
posites,
pink cockatoos,
pinheads,
perfect parents,
popes,
patriarchs,
patricides,
paraplegics,
pipsqueaks,
psychotics,
prescribed psychoanalytic paths,
phallic theories, resolved mental
problems, dialectical
poles, split
personalities and
philosopher's stones, or at least the
primal matter needed to
produce them.

7

Staying home turned out to be the right thing to do. Now that something had come out of his *thing*, Dane felt edgy despite Dr Petrossian's reassuring news. He needed time to process what Jess had said. She must see what was happening to him as some sort of pregnancy, even though she knew that a man couldn't be pregnant. Jess, however, generally more open-minded and risk-friendly than he was, had a much broader concept of 'giving birth' than he did. Of 'begetting'. 'Spawning'. 'Producing'. 'Bearing'. 'Creating'. 'Generating'. 'Engendering'. 'Authoring'. There were so many words for it. What about 'hosting'?

The fact was that Jessica longed for children, a girl first, then a boy. The earth, hosting another child. An ant wasn't a child. But that wasn't the issue. Do you kill what your body hosts: that was the question. Dane knew well that he was some kind of planet to billions of bacteria, which kept him alive. They lived through him, and he lived through them. Wasn't it the same with the earth? Weren't all the creatures hosted by Mother Earth, in some way or another, beneficial to her? Except maybe *Homo sapiens*.

Dane could feel a headache coming on, and he was unusually thirsty. He brewed more Guaya'b for Jess, but poured a pitcher of water for himself.

You're clammy, she said. Do you have a fever?

I don't think so.

Let's take your temp.

After only a few seconds the thermometer under his tongue beeped. 37 °C. That's normal, isn't it?

Jess looked up 'normal body temperature' on her tablet, just to make sure. Yes, that's normal. She smiled. Do you feel dizzy?

He shook his head.

Nauseated?

No.

She shrugged. Is your stomach upset? Do your joints ache?

Dane suffered from none of that; what he sometimes suffered from was Jess coming home from Hygiene History, asking all sorts of questions about his bodily functions. Hygiene was enough, but Health was too much.

Headache?

He nodded. It doesn't really hurt though. More like a droning.

A buzz?

More like a hum. He tried to imitate it but failed.

Jess looked it up. That's cranial.

Is that serious?

Not necessarily, according to the International Headache Society. Jess put her tablet away. But I think you should call in sick today.

Dane didn't like that suggestion. Saturday night, as Jess very well knew, was Gulo Gulo's big night. Although the restaurant insisted on treating every guest as a VIP, real VIPs tended to come in greater numbers on Saturdays. For tonight, three celebrity guests had signalled a potential appearance. Three *independent* celebs and their parties, meaning, three *best* tables had to be reserved, whether they showed or not. Dane didn't envy Lofty Liu his job. If they didn't turn up, Lofty had to resort to his list of sit-ins, that is, guests who could come on short notice and fill the seats. The sight of an empty table on a Saturday evening could ruin the other diners' appetites and permanently damage the restaurant's rep. Some of these sit-ins even looked a bit like celebrities and all behaved charmingly entitled like them. It was customary for the no-show celebs to pick up the tab for these sit-ins; it was, however, often a bitch to get them to ante up. No, Dane didn't envy Lofty Liu. Envy in general, like jealousy, wasn't in Dane's character.

I feel better already, Dane said, watching her feather-dust the tchotchkes on the bedroom windowsill: a set of miniature drums, a tiny Colombian tour bus with the word RIO-NEGRO painted on its side (a gift from a friend who'd visited Bogotá), a Gimme! coffee cup, and the silver medal Dane won for his neri at the AFC Northeast Regional Conference in Providence, RI, among other things.

Finally Dane decided that he would go to work but stay in bed until it was time to get ready. Jess continued to busy herself with the multi-coloured feather duster she had given him as a Valentine Day's present a few years ago. Although Dane didn't consider dusting a specifically female chore – he was usually the one doing it – he welcomed that Jessica finally applied something she'd learned in her Hygiene History course to the reality of their apartment.

Changing into his antipasto chef clothes in Gulo Gulo's green room, Dane discovered three more ants on his belly. Naturally, his first impulse was to kill them; his second to think of them as newborns and give them names. As all three were relentlessly stumbling over each other, he named them Larry, Moe and Curly. It felt like the right thing to do, male impulse giving way to female instinct, something Jessica could have said. It was a nice confirmation of Dane's decision that one of the celebrity guests who showed that night was the guy who played Curly in the remake of *The Three Stooges*.

This served to increase Dane's enthusiasm about his own tiny trio. On breaks, however, watching the babies learn so quickly how to circle on his body without bumping into each other made him realize how inappropriately he'd named them. He wished he had his mother's confidence: although in the beginning he didn't look like a Dane at all, she'd simply known one day he'd grow into one. How proud his mother would be if she could see him now! Dane carefully pulled down his undershirt and chef smock and went back to work. Each time he went to the bathroom, he found more ants crawling around on his belly.

Bubblegum, bubblegum, eight, twelve, fifteen, he hummed.

A FELLOW WRITER TOLD me that he envies me for sitting, for *having* to sit, for not being able to constantly run away, for *having* to write. I mumble something about the medical side effects of all that sitting, but when it comes to writing, the guy is dead on, isn't he?

COULDN'T RESERVE A SEAT in a sold-out movie theatre even though there were several spots available in the wheelchair. When I called they told me there was nothing they could do: the system doesn't count the wheelchair spots. Sold out for the abled, it's sold out for the disabled as well.

Progressive:
I am a lot of work.

Update:
I'm even more work now.

Jan:
But you're good work!

Vertigo
by Les Murray

Last time I fell in a shower-room
I bled like a tumbril dandy
and the hotel longed to be rid of me.
Taken to the town clinic, I
described how I tripped on a steel
rim and found my head in a wardrobe.
Scalp-sewn and knotted and flagged
I thanked the Frau Doktor and fled,
wishing the grab-bar of age might
be bolted to all civilization
and thinking of Rome's eighth hill
heaped up out of broken amphorae.

When, any time after sixty,
or any time before, you stumble
over two stairs and club your forehead
among rake or hoe, brick or fuel-tin,
that's time to call the purveyor
of steel pipe and indoor railings
and soon you'll be gasping up landings
having left your balance in the car
from which please God you'll never see
the launchway of tyres off a brink.
Later comes the sunny day when
street detail gets whitened to mauve

and people hurry you, or wait, quiet.

I MET LES MURRAY IN 1999 in Frauenfeld, Switzerland, when he was reading at a poetry festival. Here he was, the most dignified, compassionate, sharpest and funniest poet of the other (but shouldn't all poets be poets of The Other?) – the most human of them all – the sayer of what's right in this unjust world where you get sacked for being different (or, more likely, not hired to begin with). He had just written the novel-in-verse *Fredy Neptune*, about a twentieth-century, working-class-hero reimagining of Ulysses, shocked into disability by the sight of Armenian women drenched in kerosene and forced to dance, living torches, for the entertainment of their Turkish murderers. ('These eyes of mine – / How shall I dig the eyes out, how shall I, how?' – from Siamanto's epigraph to *Fredy Neptune*.) Fredy develops superpowers that are questionable, as superpowers generally are: he stops feeling pain (Fredy calls it his 'numb talent') and starts developing superhuman strength, bending iron and lifting freight cars.

SO THERE I WAS, drinking a glass of milk with Fredy's creator (Les later denied that that was all he was drinking). Then, just as weight-defying as his creation, he carried me on his back up the heavy stairs to where he was giving his reading. And what a reading he gave! He fully embodied his poetry – a little breathlessly, I thought, perhaps because he'd just carried me up a flight of stairs. Ever since, when he's in New York, we eat sweetbread together (he did, I had pork chops), go for (very short) city walks, pee in robber baron mansions (he did, I used the bathroom). Les travels a lot, I not so much any more.

Les, who has meanwhile left this earth, who now eats sweetbread with God and pees in the atrium of Him to whose glory all his books are dedicated, was the bravest of men, with so many ailments, health problems, disabilities, all of which he wrote about – just for me, I sometimes imagine when I'm reading you, dear faraway friend.

Dear Andrew Solomon,

We've just received another of your group emails regarding our PEN membership renewal. As you haven't yet found the time to answer our letter sent to your office on March 20, allow us to send it to you again.

Rest assured, my wife, Jan Heller Levi, and I will renew our membership as soon as PEN will finally include as explicit policy the protection of the basic rights of its members (and not just members) with disabilities. To deny access to people in wheelchairs (or not provide sign language translators, etc.), as it has happened at PEN-organized events, is a serious violation of freedom of speech.

This is personal: due to a progressive neuromuscular disability called Spinal Muscular Atrophy (type III), I'm in a wheelchair, a fact that has repeatedly excluded me from PEN events as they were hosted in inaccessible venues. My several attempts to draw PEN's attention to this problem (including a letter to a former PEN President) have remained unanswered. (Whether a PEN event is accessible to everybody usually isn't indicated on the PEN website.)

As a result of that, my wife and I have stayed away from all PEN activities, including the accessible ones. Which, I'm sure, is the majority. But in much the same way you can't make exceptions when it comes to freedom of speech, so you can't make exceptions when it comes to universal access.

Best wishes,
Christoph Keller & Jan Heller Levi

MBONGWANA STAR, a Congolese band, has two lead singers in wheelchairs. Name one Western band with two lead singers in wheelchairs. Name two Western bands with one leadsinger in a wheelchair. Name any Western band with anyone in a wheelchair.

ON THE PLANE, trying to get the remote control out of the arm-rest of my seat. No can do; nor can Jan. The flight attendant offers to get it out with her 'tiny fingers' (her words), but another flight attendant, maybe realizing that this is too intimate a procedure for everyone involved, tells her to get a knife. I don't like the sound of that, but what can I do? I want to watch something; I certainly don't want to sit there watching everyone else watch something for the next nine hours, pressed against the gadget that would allow me to join this motley flying crew of watchers. So I lean over to the right side as much as I can. There is literally zero room between my thigh and the armrest. (Yes, I had asked for a move-able armrest, and yes, they are obliged by law to give me a seat with one.) When they return with a knife, I lean over, close my eyes and try not to think of surgery. Instead I think of when we were on another plane. Five flight attendants tried to lift the arm-rest so it would be easier to transfer me to the aisle chair. They couldn't do it; they had to call an engineer. So we waited for an engineer to come to perform the surgery (with tiny tools) to lift the armrest. Do we require an engineer now? No, combining their powers, the two flight attendants manage to dislodge the remote control, embedded in my armrest like a malignant tumour. The female attendant hands the gadget to me with an embarrassed smile. The male one sighs. I watch five episodes of *Veep*, drink two small whiskeys, sleep for two hours, read a little, worry about whether my wheelchair will survive the trip intact.

TODAY I'M READING in the paper about how real estate agents direct black people to black neighbourhoods, Latinos to Latino neighbourhoods, whites to white neighbourhoods. I'm also reading an essay by the poet Jenny Zhang about how it feels when a white guy assumes a Chinese-sounding name in order to get published (shitty) and about 'white flight' Asian-style: unlike African Americans, causing 'violence to rise and schools to fail', Asians moving into your white neighbourhood is no good because they cause schools to become too *excellent*. I'm thinking of Jan's and my letter to PEN, stubbornly sent and re-sent to the organization's president, by email (to different addresses), by snail mail. How does it feel *not* to get an answer to a letter asking for exclusively accessible venues, even from your own organization? Discriminatory? That's not a feeling. Awful. Horrible. Another non-feeling comes to mind: unnecessary. They don't even bother, comes to mind. They don't give a shit, comes to mind. So this is how it feels: shitty. As it is in the poetry world, so it is with everything: the powerful, still mostly able-bodied male whites, in Jenny Zhang's words, 'scramble to come up with ways to keep the playing field uneven, to keep the odds stacked in their favour.'

3rd Ave & 9th St

BUG STORY

8

Sunday to Tuesday were Dane's days off, and Dane and Jess didn't leave their apartment. Jess even skipped her free Monday lunchbreak class at Tibet House, which this Monday was about levitation, and neither she nor Dane bothered to go downstairs to get the mail. It was too much of a miracle to watch the ants hatch out of Dane's thing. Dane felt that she still didn't entirely trust him to be left alone with the newborns. But as they grew in numbers, and as he spent more time with them, his urge to kill them ebbed away. By Tuesday evening, the ants were in the hundreds.

I guess we have to stop counting, Jessica said, who, as a result of her suburban upbringing, was much more patient than Dane. He'd already given up. What's most important is that they're healthy.

The growing number of ants made it easier to study their habits. Jess watched the activity on Dane's belly for a long time.

They're single-minded creatures, incredibly focused, determined, fair to each other and loyal, she declared earnestly.

It was fascinating to watch how tirelessly they moved on his skin. The small creatures moved systematically, always in circles and without ever bumping into each other. Each circle intersected with the circles of its neighbours. Speedy, but elegant, the ants, in constant motion, slipped past their brothers or sisters; each circle had a diameter of approximately an inch; to complete a full circle took an ant approximately a second, which was – Jess tapped on her phone calculator – 60 circles a minute, 3,600 an hour, 86,400 a day, 604,800 a week and 220,752,000 circles a year.

Dizzying, Dane said.

Do you know how long ants live?

A few months max.

Jess's face darkened.

Maybe even a few years?

There's so much about life we don't know, Dane.

He closed his eyes. Although it was only 9 p.m., he was tired. At the same time he could tell that it'd be hard to fall asleep with so much to think about. For starters, what was happening to him? He produced the ants, yes, but what produced them in him? Was it something he ate, as Jess once suggested? Something he breathed in or had contracted, maybe even from Jess? Could you tell these days what produced what? Did we, in the already age-ing twenty-first century, still live in a cause-and-effect world?

Now that there were so many things interacting with so many other things, was it really still possible to say what was the effect and what the cause? Companies, for instance, were all too aware of the unpredictability of cause and effect. They now sometimes made you (the consumer) sign a document of indemnification before you were granted the privilege of buying their products. Could you blame them? How was it the company's fault when all a company did was provide a product so many people (including you!) all of a sudden couldn't live without any more? Wanting may be part of the pursuit of happiness but it isn't risk-free.

Only recently had Jess come home with a new and improved set of hair removal razor blade cartridges she'd very much looked forward to trying out. But while struggling with the stiff packaging, she cut herself *and* damaged the product. Once her anger had subsided and her wrist had stopped bleeding, Jess agreed that the guilty party wasn't the maker of a product that had provided her with so much enthusiasm; nor was it the maker of the pack-aging who'd done nothing but try protecting her from herself. No, the guilty party was *she*, the consumer, who'd been carried away by her unbridled enthusiasm.

It was a truly mind-boggling argument. It was a topsy-turvy world they lived in.

Tipsy-turvy, Jess liked to say.

This made Dane smile, dozing away a bit.

You look so happy when you're asleep, Jess said, apparently still in the bedroom.

Without opening his eyes, Dane smiled for her.

Wasn't it even more 'tipsy-turvy' for him? After all, he was on both sides of this conundrum of modern civilization. On the one hand, as a consumer, a dining patron, for example, he didn't want to be blamed for needing the restaurant products; on the other hand, as someone who was providing the much-needed product (food), he wanted even less to take any blame when providing it.

Really, how could one know what would happen to Guest X when brought into contact with Product Y? Did he, Dane, always anticipate what would happen to a taste (or a guest) when he experimented with a new selection of ingredients? What it came down to was this: it was a trial-and-error world, a world that came with unwelcome side effects, whether one liked it or not.

He'd been grateful, however, when LMC introduced an indemnification policy. Of course, LMC was fully aware of what the food served in his several restaurants could potentially do to the mainly upper-class and thus extremely sensitive digestive systems of his guests. Everyone who wanted to enjoy the benefits of his dining establishments had to sign the document before being served. It was risky at first, but, like every reasonable revolution, it caught on and even became a cool asset after only a few derisive comments from the New York City food critics. Practically all his guests signed, agreeing that it was their fault, not the restaurant's, if they ate something that disagreed with them.

Now these documents circulated, signed and laminated, on eBay (so far the Mayor's had generated the highest bid); hipster Park Slope intellectuals produced them in the midst of an argument (no matter what the argument was about); and one had even been spotted hanging in a gilded frame in the waiting room of Dr Dennie Denner, prominent Upper East Side shrink to the stars.

(*The mailroom of our building.* CHRISTOPH *is getting mail.* LARRY
KRAMER, *who also lives in the building, enters. They know each
other from* CHRISTOPH's *work in the building library. A year ago,*
LARRY – b. 1935, *author of the play* The Normal Heart *and the gar-
gantuan novel* The American People, *human rights activist,
legendary gadfly and certified Very Difficult Man – had been placed
in a wheelchair, by the autoimmune disease he dedicated his life to
fighting politically.* LARRY *used to walk down the back stairway that
leads to the library. Although he can't do that any more, instead riding the elevator, he is back on his feet, using a walker that sits in the
entrance to the mailroom, in everybody's way,* LARRY-style.)

— What's it like to be in a wheelchair?
— It's a pain in the ass.
— How long have you been in the chair?
— I got my first one when I was twenty-five. When I could still
walk a mile or so.
— When's the last time you stood?
— Maybe five years ago. I have Spinal Muscular Atrophy.
— Never heard of it. What is it comparable to?
— Muscular Dystrophy. It's in the family of Lou Gehrig's ALS, but
less brutal. With a normal life expectancy.
— How do you go to the bathroom?
— I pee in a plastic bottle. I empty the bottle into the toilet.
— But pooping? How do you poop?
— I use a commode. I wrote a book about all this.
— Is it a novel?
— It's a memoir. A memoir-novel, actually. I'll leave a copy for you
at the desk.
— I'll leave a pile of my books for you at the desk.

(LARRY *grabs his walker and exits.* CHRISTOPH *follows slowly in
his wheelchair.*)

TONIGHT I'M DREAMING of my oldest brother. He's thin, standing firmly. There's no wheelchair. He's walking. What does this mean, dream? I've a hard time remembering my brother thin, or either one of my brothers walking. When I dream of myself I'm never in a wheelchair. I'm always thin. I'm standing, firmly. I'm walking, blissfully. So what are you about, dream? Can we all walk in dreams? Is all we need for walking a parallel world? No. This dream is for Larry Kramer, who made it out of the wheelchair and back onto his own two feet in real life. For Larry Kramer, who meanwhile has also left this earth – or maybe not, as he will certainly find a way to keep fighting for justice.

Larry, my walking brother.

Cream

In the waiting room of the Muscle
Clinic at Columbia-Presbyterian,
thinking of the pictures of my ass
rash on my phone. Other people
have pictures of their kids and cute
pets. Who wants to see *those*? But
my doctor really wants to see the
pictures of my ass rash to prescribe
a cool cream.

BEFORE WE VISIT Anne Marie and Jerry's new apartment, she measures the doors to make sure they're wide enough. My chair, with its motors in its wheels, requires more room than others. The width of a regular wheelchair for adults is 26″. Mine is 27.8″. ADA minimum for a door is 32″, but many doors don't meet that requirement, especially in New York, where every inch counts, especially in pre-war buildings like this one. Anne Marie's eager for me to test the doors, and I'm eager to put them to the test. She gives me the feeling that if I can't get through them, it will be the doors who fail the test, not me.

WHEN THEY TELL YOU they're sorry that you feel that way, you know they know you're right. You also know they don't want to do anything about it.

TODAY I'M WRITING, as I sometimes do, in the shadow of Fiorello's statue on LaGuardia Place, when a woman with a big yellow dogs stops a foot away from me. The big yellow dog makes a choking noise.

'Is he all right?' I ask.

'Stomach problems,' she says and sighs.

The big yellow dog leans over and throws up yellow stuff in front of me. One spin of my wheels, and I'd be sitting in it. The woman says nothing. Does she think I'm just another statue?

Yellow stuff keeps coming out of the big yellow dog. The woman waits patiently. When the big yellow dog starts licking the yellow stuff he's just thrown up, I finally give in and roll away.

MOST NORTH AMERICAN INDIGENOUS communities don't have a word or a concept for 'disability'. This is because their communities once thrived on identifying each person's talent. Someone with a mental impairment is good at carrying water, she who is deaf is a great builder of huts, he who is paralysed is a born story-teller. As long as the relationship of body, spirit and mind is in balance, there is no 'disability'. Enter the Europeans on their ships with guns, rum, Bibles, greed and viruses; enter capitalism bringing ashore the concept of 'disability'.

WHEN THEY TELL YOU you're bitter when you say that something feels liberating and incredibly right to you, you're on to something.

— HOW DOES IT FEEL?

— It doesn't.

— But how can something so big, a *thing* so defining –

— Not hurt?

— Of course, it's great that it doesn't . . .

— Yet, sometimes I wish it did. But no, there's nothing. No pain. How can you describe loss when it doesn't hurt?

— You're asking me?

— You can put pain on a map. You can point and say, Look, here, that's where it hurts. You can touch that spot. You know where it is. I can't do that.

— So, in a way, it's everywhere.

— And nowhere. SMA is a colonizer. It colonizes the voluntary muscles. You know, the ones that make your arms and legs move. The ones that move you around. It pretty much leaves alone the involuntary muscles.

— So, again, it's a good thing . . .

— What do you mean?

— . . . that it's not the involuntary ones that are being colonized.

— Yep, definitely. That's the heart, the stomach, the intestines. It gets a little tricky when it gets to the lung muscles. Breathing is a combination of voluntary and involuntary muscles.

— So what does that mean for you?

— Like so often, I have to wait and see.

SOMETIMES I THINK because SMA doesn't hurt it is imaginary. I have a waking dream that if I were startled out of my sleep because the house was on fire, I'd *forget*, jump out of bed, grab Jan, and together we'd run from the building.

THE MOST POWERFUL superhero I've invented so far is Commonsenseman. His Kryptonite is that no one listens to him.

Washington Square West & Washington Pl

BUG STORY

9

At some point on Wednesday, Jess, coming home from her shift at the Gap while Dane was mentally preparing for his own at Gulo Gulo, noticed something peculiar. If she stood far away enough from Dane, say at one end of the living room while he stood at the other, she couldn't see the little creatures move; she actually couldn't see them at all. Their unceasing communal motion tricked the eye and the ants became a static mass, a yellow-brownish weave of semi-transparent protein.

It reminded her of a show she'd seen at MOMA – or was it the Met? – of paintings that were very different depending on whether you stood close or far away. If you were too close all you saw was paint; but if you moved far enough away you saw a pond with water lilies. It was fascinating, beautiful in a hallucinatory sense, Jess thought. Anyway, from a distance, it looked as though Dane were wearing a second skin, one darker than his primary skin, less Lower East Side and more Colombian, like hers. It also made her think of the light brown wool sweaters they had on sale at the Gap. With so many ants moving on his body so fast and systematically, in countless overlapping circles, Dane looked naked and clothed at the same time.

Look, Jess said.

I've got to get ready.

Just a sec. Stand in front of the hallway mirror. And now step back.

He did. Cool, he said. I'll wear something loose for work today so I don't hurt the ants.

In a way Jess, who chose clothes by touch as much as by look, regretted that, likely, she'd no longer be doing that for Dane.

She liked touching Dane as much as she liked touching cashmere, which comforted her, or silk, which excited her.

It's cold.

The ants keep you warm.

They do, don't they? Warm when it's cold, cool when it's hot. I'm always at just the right temperature.

And nothing hurts?

Dane shook his head. It tickles, throbs and tingles.

Feels good?

Feels hot.

Hot-hot or sexy-hot?

Hot-hot-sexy-hot.

Oh, darling. Your ants are so close to you – I'm jealous! Jess kissed him on a small antfree spot on his chest just above the left nipple. Change is hard, she thought. Change is bittersweet. But Dane was her future; given the sorry state mankind was in, he may even be everybody's future. She kissed him again, closer to the circling ants, more soulfully and longer, carefully fondling some of Dane's unsettled territories, all the while making sure not to crush any of the fragile creatures.

We shouldn't, Dane said.

I'll be careful, darling, Jess said.

You know what, Jess said, a little later, vacuuming. It was amazing how far under the bed the vacuum cleaner's nozzle reached! She was aware that she was a bit of an obsessive person, but she hadn't foreseen that she'd be so into cleaning all of a sudden. Change was hard but also rewarding. She was changing with Dane, changing for Dane, while Dane was changing for her. She turned off the vacuum cleaner.

What?

I don't have any.

What do you mean?

Look. What is it you don't see on my body?

He saw flip-flops, short-shorts and her (and his) favourite pink tanktop. He saw her smooth, perfect skin. Lots of it. Then he understood.

Ants, he said.

Wouldn't it be natural for them to migrate? Colonize me as well? Keep expanding their territory? Why don't they?

He wrinkled his brow a little. Are you disappointed? . . . Worried? he added when she didn't answer.

You should be, Jess said. It means your ants can't leave you but I can.

Will you, Jessica?

Never, she said and looked around. The apartment looked, and smelled, so clean, ready for them to move in again.

On Thursday, Dane worked the lunch shift at Gulo, and Jess attended a lecture at the New School that was part of her History of Hygiene course. Afterwards, Jess prepared a deliriously delicious fettuccine all'arrabiata with barely any help from Dane. Dane wasn't hungry. He ate just enough so as not to offend the cook.

What do you think my ants eat?

Jess looked at him. You. I think.

And where do you think they do their business?

On you, I guess, she said and laughed.

Yikes, he said. To shit where you eat is the biggest no-no in the food world!

Don't make too much of it, she said. Think of your body as a restaurant. A place where you do all of that.

Dane stared at her in disbelief. But there are *walls*, Jess!

Well, do you see the ants eat?

He shook his head.

Do you see them shit?

No, Dane said.

Well, then maybe you also don't see the walls, do you?

Dane said nothing.

Jess had looked up Dane's ants on her tablet. From what she could tell, the ones Dane was growing were 'pioneer ants', a small (2 mm) yellow or light brown species, almost transparent, and notorious as a major indoor nuisance, especially in hospitals and apartment buildings.

They're good at colonizing, Jess said. They have many queens. Queen ants can fly, so they're constantly building new colonies. They're good at foraging. They also clean themselves a lot.

That's good, Dane said.

Don't spray them, Jess said. They only scatter.

I thought we're beyond killing them.

I'm just reading what it says here, she said. But not everything you read online is true. Look at this. She tapped on her tablet to make the typeface larger. Here's what they eat. Things like jelly, peanut butter, anything baked, fruit juice, but also toothpaste, shoe polish and dead insects.

Dead insects?

Maybe themselves once they're dead. Maybe even before they're dead.

Cannibal ants?

What do I know.

Don't be macabre, Dane said.

Ecological, Dane, Jess said. I'm ecological. But I'm very impressed by you. Very.

She let her finger hover over the colony on his belly. There was a sort of regrouping, and when Jess placed her finger gently on his belly, there was a bit of a commotion, even panic in the community. Yet quickly, the little intelligent animals adapted to the new situation, adjusting their circling to the change in terrain. And yes, Jess was right, they devoured the ones that didn't survive the attack.

Cruel, Dane said.

Purposeful, she said. They feed on their own. No waste. They self-compost, so to speak. But what is it, darling? You look upset.

So far I can hide my ants underneath my clothes. So far they haven't reached my hands or my feet. Or my neck. My face. He hesitated. But what happens if they do? What will happen if the ants reach my mouth, Jess? He shuddered. And what about my ears? My nostrils?

He stopped, took a deep breath. My ass?

Your orifices, Jess said, using the term preferred in Hygiene class.

Orifices, Dane repeated. But still, what'll happen to me?

I don't know. Let's cross that bridge when we get to it.

Tunnel, he said. Those are not bridges but tunnels leading inside me.

Neither of them slept well that night.

Dane dreamed that he was spitting out entire platoons of ants, plucking them out of his nostrils and ears and other orifices. When he couldn't take it any more, he reluctantly resorted to what was now against his nature and sprayed the invading ants as fast as he could. They scattered but he didn't care. He just kept spraying, spraying, spraying.

Jess had a similar dream. Realizing how Dane suffered from the ant invasion, she picked them as quickly and carefully as she could from his body and gave them shelter on her own, where they settled peacefully. For a while she felt good – wasn't she a better host to this ant colony than Dane would ever be? – but then she saw what that had done to Dane: he was lying next to her, gasping his last breath, without an inch of skin on his body, just a bloody mess of muscles, nerves and bones.

MY FRIEND HEINRICH KUHN AND I have written three novels together. Today, we're launching our fourth book, a collection of very short stories called *Everything Else Will Take Care of Itself*. The book launch takes place in St Gallen. I'm at my desk in New York, Skyped-in. It's just after 8 p.m. there, that is, just after 2 p.m. here. The way the computer is set up I can't see the audience, but judging from the audio the room is packed. What I see is a window, and through the window I see one of St Gallen's hills, the Mountain of Joy (the other one is called the Mountain of Roses; don't you want to move there?). Looking up from my computer, I see the West Village, glimpses of the Hudson, the vast horizon over New Jersey, in broad daylight. Looking down again, I see the Swiss daylight slowly fading. I'm not surprised that several of the texts I've chosen to read talk about clouds and skies.

MY FIRST WIFE kept saying there was nothing I did wrong, it was just over. She wanted to leave. Yet she didn't. I kept pressing her. I needed to hear why. Why? *You're such a good guy, it's just –* It's just *what*? So finally she said it. It's because you can't go skiing with me. It's because you're not strong enough in bed. It's because – I want other positions as well. There, she said it. Happy now? It was devastating. It was good. It was honest. Strangely, she still didn't leave. We even had weak sex. She was right: It wasn't good. Finally, I asked her to leave. If you want to go, go now. It was what she needed to hear.

If ever I lose my legs, I won't have to walk no more.
    (C. S.)

MY FATHER SAID HE DRANK because he couldn't deal with having three disabled sons. His idea of manliness was John Wayne. Guns and horses. He loved Westerns, and so did I. We watched a lot of them together when I was a kid, he drunk, I, as far away from him as possible, hunkered down in a very low lounge chair. I was aware that we were watching what he thought were real men.

Sometimes he said, 'The doctors are all wrong. My sons are not cripples.'

Sometimes he said, 'Cripples can't be the heirs of my business.'

(Maybe he secretly considered us superheroes but just couldn't say it out loud.)

But you can ignore a progressive disability only for so long. I wonder now whether that was why my father fought so much with my oldest brother. Because he couldn't bear watching his first son, the designated heir, grow into a cripple. I stopped watching Westerns with my father when two things became excessively obvious: first, how hard it was getting to be to lift myself from that lounge chair; and second, how drunk he was every night.

Did I mention that my father never sat on a horse? He did own guns, though. Plenty of them. One went off when he was showing my mother how safe guns were. He didn't hit her. The bullet went so close to her right ear that she suffered permanent hearing loss.

Meanwhile, the designated heir, unable to brandish a gun, ride a horse or even, as time went by, lift an arm, went on to build a highly profitable business from what he rescued from the scraps of his father's bankrupt company.

BUT WHEN YOU ALREADY have two of those, wouldn't it have been better to not have a third one? a neighbour said with the unquestionable authority of the impeccably healthy man to my mother after I was born.

THE OTHER DAY A mother of three told me how glad she is that her youngest daughter, with all her mental health problems, *doesn't* have a child. 'What kind of unhealthy child would that be?' This mother of three asked me this, sitting in front of me, in the living room of my mother, another mother of three.

NO WHEELCHAIR SPACE in Cooper Union's Great Hall, where Lincoln once gave his famous speech. I sit in front of the first-row seats. I'm my own row of one seat. Anne Marie sits with me, that is, behind me. Everybody else sits wherever they want. I'm a fire hazard. Let them come and tell me that, I say to her, *and I'll put it in my book!*

Nobody does.

The tribute to Philip Levine, beautiful and sad.

Most moving when Jerry, who is the last speaker, slowly shuffles his chair backwards, getting half up, shuffling backwards, sitting down, getting half up again, shuffling closer and closer towards to edge of the stage. Any second his great friend will appear on the big screen and read a poem. I worry Jerry might fall off the stage. I get ready to jump out of my wheelchair so I can hold him.

I know I could.

I know I could.

I know I could.

The man on the screen starts reading, large and in colour, me watching his great friend, a silhouette with hat on a chair, from behind, watching his great friend read 'Burial Rites': *Everyone comes back here to die / as I will soon.*

If My Body (Second ConEd Poem)

All my life I've struggled to explain
what exactly it is that I have. A muscle-
wasting disease, as my first doctor said?
It always sounded wrong to me.

A progressive neuromuscular disease?
That's what science says. SMN-2 is what
science calls the defect gene; what it does
is waste muscles. Mine. But I have them.

Ever since I call myself a writer, I wonder:
Do I have a communication disorder? My muscles
hear less and less what my brain tells them to do,
and therefore they're wasted, progressively.

Is that it? So if my body were a house,
my brain would be the main panel,
right under the electric meter.
My nerves would be the rusty wires,

getting rustier. And even though
I always pay my ConEd bill on time,
the lights – my movements – would flicker
progressively, and then go out.

Ok, writer. What then in your house
would be your muscles? Unable to hear
the commands of the light switches,
they'd have no place in this metaphor.

AFTER MY DIAGNOSIS I started watching my body more closely. I was thirteenish. I was mostly concerned with my unruly bangs and my slightly bulging belly. The former I glued in place with Scotch tape overnight, hoping they would stay there without the tape during the day. They didn't. My bulging belly was a side effect of my SMA, not of my being overweight. I was skinny. My muscles, weakening, couldn't hold in place the weight I was naturally putting on as a teenager. No washboard abs for me. I obsessed about losing weight anyway, in binges, so to speak. The result was pointy shoulders that showed off my bones, not my muscles.

10

On Friday, Dane had a lunch date with his friend Gale. Gale Force was a leftover from his pre-Jessica days, which Gale half-jokingly referred to as Dane's pre-Columbian days. In a spirit of open-mindedness Jess tried not to be retroactively jealous. Dane had assured her that it had been nothing, really, just a fling; or not even that: it was all a blur in the distant past now.

At least for him. For Jess, though, it was hard to live with Gale Force regularly intruding on her life. Now she couldn't decide whether she wanted Gale to accept Dane's new condition or be repelled by it. Either scenario was unsettling to her.

I was drunk, he said, skipping the rest of the monthly semi-fight they had before he saw Gale.

Go, she finally said, as she always did.

It was true that he did discuss things with Gale he didn't bring up with Jessica, such as daring new recipes or having children. It was strange. With Gale he didn't want children but wanted to talk about having them, and with Jess he wanted to have children but didn't want to talk about it. He concluded he wasn't entirely ready, but figured this issue would probably resolve itself once he and Jess were married, with Gale remaining his best woman friend.

Like Jess, however, he also wondered how Gale would react to his new condition. Unlike Jess, he was quite certain that she'd understand; his concern, frankly, was that Gale might be *more* understanding than Jessica. That is, maybe not more, but *differently* understanding. Even if he were with Gale, he couldn't imagine her calling his ants 'theirs', and certainly not 'hers'. If there was one thing Gale wasn't it was possessive. That was why he was with Jessica Moreno and not Gale Force.

Dane, wearing one of Jess's kimonos, that being the

loosest-fitting piece of clothing they could find, checked on his ants. They were doing fine. They had settled Dane's entire belly, his chest and parts of his shoulders. Previously, there had been something of a distinguishable frontier line; but now it seemed that the colonization process had broken into separate settlements. Some ants had created outposts in his armpits and on his back, and there was a southwards movement too, some ants exploring the wilderness of Dane's hairy groin. Jess helped Dane choose a long-sleeved and somewhat ant-coloured shirt and a pair of loose linen pants.

I'll walk you. I have to pick up some things at Agata & Valentina anyway. And then I'm off to the Gap. You know, Kira, the manager, has made noises about promoting me to Assistant Sales Manager.

Seriously?

Just before yesterday's shift was over I turned a disgruntled customer into a likely returning one. All it took was for me to exchange a non-exchangeable item, a grey zip-fronted hoodie, with Kanga pockets that, admittedly, didn't do much to improve the customer's slightly froggish face.

That's so great, Jess! Dane kissed her. Dearest Jessica!

Yess, she said. From now on, for you, Yess, and for everybody else Yessica. This is the beginning of the new me! The real me! From now on I'll take care of you the way you took care of me. I've always believed in you, and now I believe in you even more. How are our ants today, darling?

We're good, Jess. He resisted the urge to scratch the back of his right knee, where some ants were now building some outposts.

Yess, Yess said.

Yess.

Where are you having lunch with Gale?

At Le Lapin Enragé.

Ooh-la-la, Mr Fancy-Pants.

I'll eat what I can.

Bring the rest home in a doggy-bag.

As Dane walked down University Place, the ants tickled him a bit. The *promozioni* at A&V looked as delicious as always, and Yess convinced him to duck in with her for a look before heading over to lunch with Gale. Yess ducked in with more gusto than usual. The promozioni-antipasto, an exclusive casalinga caponata alla Siciliana, lived up to Dane's critical eye but, unlike Yess, he didn't have any desire to sample it. It occurred to him that he hadn't eaten since yesterday's light lunch but wasn't hungry at all; or thirsty, for that matter.

Since the Swiss was sold out, Yess snatched a chunk of gruyère reduced to $13.99/lb. 'Ghost chillis', peppers twice as hot as the hottest habaneros, had just arrived, ready to be sampled. They were the exact kind he used for his famous spaghetti neri frutti di mare piccolo. Dane reined in his curiosity. A single bite would create torrents of sweat that the ants, whether they were familiar with that text or not, might experience as Biblical.

The trip through A&V's curated food aisles was encouragingly uneventful. People stared, but then people always stared at something, be it Dane's invitingly manly face, especially when sporting a sexy chef-stubble, or Yessica's exquisitely sculpted legs, which a connoisseur could appreciate whether she wore baggy pants or skin-hugging leggings (like now), or left her legs bare. Sometimes, Dan imagined, her bare ankles alone could cause a shop-stopping stir, sending the entire island of Manhattan back to the Victorian era. Many shopped at A&V's for the sole reason that they could count on seeing people like Yessica and Dane there; again, Dane's mother had it right when she said that one ate first with one's eyes.

But when Dane, insisting on managing the money transaction,

reached out to hand the cashier his credit card, his sleeve slipped back just a bit to expose a few industrious marchers circling on his arm. Just in time, he managed to pull down his sleeve.

Once outside again, Dane pulled up his sleeve to discover that the ants had by no means erected only a small outpost near his wrist but had occupied his entire right arm. He discreetly showed Yess what had happened.

Maybe I should cancel with Gale?

Certainly not, Yess said.

Maybe I should go naked, he said half-jokingly.

Certainly not when you're seeing Gale, she said. This is no joke, Dane. This is our life now. Anyway, if you can't face a friend, how can you face anybody? And if a friend can't face you the way you are now, who can?

Gale had a choice of verdure (beets with dandelion and hazel-nuts, warm olives and eggplant caponata) followed by the restaurant's killer minestrone and, as a subtle salute to Dane, a glass of Tocai Friulano. Dane ordered two frutti di mare, calamari spermatophores and octopus carpaccio. They were both fine with tap water; neither wondered why the French-named restaur-ant specialized in Italian food.

First it was catching up, a ritual as ordinary as a heartbeat. Gale's discovery of a new gallery, someone – the name escaped her – re-creating his childhood memory from the rubble of his parents' home, which he had blown to pieces with the parents in it (the artist was working from a Pennsylvania prison). Her unpre-cedented trouble with a photo shoot for the Frequent Nautical Miles Points Program of a cruise-line company. Gale's minuscule apartment had been overflowing with bathing suits, sarongs and sandals and props like harpoons and stylish life-vests.

There was a new guy in Gale's life, too; a specimen named Frederick. Dane took an instant disliking to him. Rick – Gale refused to call him 'Fred' as all his previous lovers had done – sounded like a good match for Gale, quiet to the point of monosyllabic, a bit of a couch potato (the word 'bore' briefly hovered over their table, then dissolved). Gale was drawn to opposites. The only opposite she wasn't drawn to was living in the country. Rick, it turned out, lived upstate. She, however, was a city girl.

You're not eternally committed to this guy just because you slept with him, Dane said.

What do you think of the eggplant? It's soaked with oil.

Dane glanced at his untouched plate. This was a slippery slope. Not touching food at Le Lapin Enragé had once made Lofty Liu the subject of a viral blog entry that had permanently damaged his reputation as a neutral food arbiter. Finally, he cut a small piece and put it in his mouth.

At least it's good oil, he said.

Well, I don't know. Gale kept eating. He lives in Neversink, Sullivan County. Population: thirty-seven trees. Rick says it's the renewed contact with the primitive that makes the countryside attractive.

A cabin with a hearth, not a mansion with a range.

But with solar panels. Rick says we're all doomed.

Better to be doomed in the city.

He sees himself as a frontiersman, uncolonizing upstate New York or something.

I have frontier ants, Dane said. Pioneer ants, actually. They're colonizing me.

Rick has them too, Gale said. They're all over his house. Spray them.

They only scatter. You can't *un*colonize.

Gale took a hearty sip of her white wine and sighed. Rick told me he once stood for an entire month in the woods, trying to grow roots. Do you believe that?

I have ants, Gale, Dane said.

You already said that, Gale said.

Dane pulled up the sleeve of his right arm.

But, *Dane*, Gale said and stopped. She mechanically cut a piece of her eggplant caponata, put it in her mouth, slowly chewed, then swallowed.

It's not just my arm. Profiting from the somewhat discreet location of their table, he tugged open the collar of his shirt. See, they're also here. They're also on my belly and my back. They're up and down my legs. Gale, I'm practically the opposite of Rick: *I'm* being colonized. Remember when we read *Walden* in high school? The ants scene?

Gale, mechanically, shook her head.

That's exactly what's *not* happening, Gale! Even if you don't remember the brutal all-out ants civil war in *Walden*. What's happening on my body is an entirely peaceful process. True, it tickles a bit, but you get used to it –

The abrupt way Gale pulled up her sleeve stopped him. He half-expected that she'd show him *her* ants, but all she exposed was her watch.

That late already, she said.

It's only two, Gale.

I have to go.

No olive oil cake?

They usually sat until it was time for him to go to work. Sometimes Gale walked him to Gulo Gulo, a fact Dane so far hadn't shared with his girlfriend – it was only a few blocks.

I know, she said and signalled to the server to bring the check. It's my tooth. I have an emergency dentist appointment.

Oh. Dane buttoned his shirt and pulled down his sleeve.

It's not serious.

It's not?

I hope not. Gale laughed uncomfortably. I woke up this morning, there was this shooting pain in my mouth, and I – let me do this, she said, as the server arrived. She left the money in cash and got up.

Thanks, he said and got up too. So, I'll see you next month?

Sure, Gale said and added another five to their server's tip.

By the time the new Dane arrived at Gulo Gulo, the ants had risen out of his collar and were now migrating to his neck and parts of his left cheek. Lofty Liu was outside, blocking the entrance to the restaurant. He was holding a long stick that looked a bit like a fishing rod, reminding Dane of the contraption one of his uncles used to pluck pears in Southern Oregon's Rogue Valley, where the pear trees grow particularly high: a ten-foot-long bamboo grappler with leathery fingers so that it wouldn't damage the fruit. Dane had always been a little afraid of that uncle. Whatever the tool was, Lofty used it to keep Dane at a distance. He made sure it didn't hit his chest, though.

I heard what's going on!

What are you doing, Lofty? Stop it!

Look at you, Dane! You're a freak! You can't work here any longer!

You can't fire me. I have a condition.

I also have a condition. Who doesn't? I've got a crush on your girlfriend. How's that for a condition? Anyway, that's not why I'm firing you. I'm firing you for unprofessional behaviour. Everyone's heard you lunched at our arch-enemy's restaurant without touching the food!

Why should I eat if I'm not hungry, Lofty?

Lofty digested this. That's so inappropriate. We fight the Lapin with all we have, and now this! You want to be a chef? A chef who doesn't eat? You're out. Get disability! Because that's what you are: a cripple! And now I can tell you: I never liked your tonnarelli. They're sticky and rubbery, and your oh-so-celebrated 'neri' tastes buttery-nutty like – like –

Like *what*, Lofty?

Escamoles!

I don't even know what those are, Dane said.

Escamoles are giant ant eggs, Lofty Liu said. And you're still fired. Tell Jess to stop by anytime. I'll always have a table for her.

I GOTTA PEE. We're at The Park in Chelsea on 10th Avenue, Jan's and my favourite restaurant whenever we visit the nearby art galleries. Great burger, fun atmosphere, especially when you manage to get a table in the semi-open space where you eat under trees with birds flapping around. What a thicket of barrier ropes and posts and baby seats and tray carts and buckets and cleaning supplies I must negotiate in the wheelchair-accessible bathroom. The restaurant uses it for storage. I manage to get to the toilet, but when I'm done, swinging around, I get stuck. Something's tangled in the wheels of my chair. I sweat, I curse. I can't tell what it is that refuses to let me go. It's scary. I wiggle my chair back and forth, back and forth. I wiggle, I yell. The music in the restaurant is too loud, I realize. No one can hear me. Somehow I manage to come untangled. I roll out of the bathroom, shaking, sweating, demoralized, furious. Back at the table with my friends, I ruin the mood.

DO YOU KNOW that you don't have to have *super*powers to be a superhero? Plenty of superheroes don't have them: Iron Man, Batman, Black Widow, Hawkeye, to just name a few. They all have *powers*. And they're all obsessed with technology and the gym. A few have money. A lot of it. Which, of course, is the ultimate superpower. It's the power that buys other people's powers. Wit and kindness are powers. Patience and humour and forgiveness. All powers. Common sense, modesty, honesty, openness. And beauty. Beauty is a power, too.

Batgirl's powers are physical: she's fast, flexible, strong. But then the Joker shoots her. A shot that paralyses her, from the waist down. That happened in 1988. At DC Comics it was agreed that the Joker needed a back story. Maybe because the comic books started to feel the winds of feminism. So what's more natural than to combine those two trends – and cripple a woman? From now on, Batgirl is Oracle. Her powers are being tech-savvy and sensitive. A crippled superhero. In a superwheelchair. Still supercute. I salute the superpowerful comic book world for revealing to a mass audience that everybody is vulnerable to disability; that everything (or nothing) is normal; and that every superhero can be a cripple.

BATGIRL'S METAMORPHOSIS, however, isn't over. Someone at DC Comics decided that it was time to get rid of the disability. So Oracle undergoes surgery and, *bada bing*, re-emerges as non-paralysed to take up her able-bodied, crime-fighting duties once more. Good for Batgirl, bad for Oracle. Because Oracle's gone. And Batgirl gets her old powers back: fast, flexible, strong. What gets thrown under the wheelchair are Oracle's powers: resilience, resourcefulness, self-sufficiency despite it all, patience, humour, depth of character, a mind stretching out into the world.

Speaking of wheelchairs: What happened to Oracle's wheelchair?

Don your cape and roll, SMA-Man!

THE METAMORPHOSIS II: 'As the monstrous bug was waking up one morning from uneasy dreams, it found itself on its lair changed into an ordinary travelling salesman named Gregor Samsa.'

Etc.

So it was now safe to say that monsters weren't being born any more . . .
But also those who were bearably sick, in a manner of speaking, ceased
to exist . . . Lichtenberg, gnome, sporting a hump, not born any more.
Neither was insane and short-lived Mozart. Beethoven didn't suffer
from deafness as he didn't exist. And Schubert? Gone, not healthy.
Likewise Nietzsche, Toulouse-Lautrec, Kafka and Thomas Bernhard.
    (H. K.)

ONE OF MY SUPERPOWERS is a Zen-like calm. I have the ability to sit at a busy Manhattan street corner and watch you rush by on your two quick legs. Sit when you sit, the Zen masters say, so I sit. And watch. The longer I sit and watch, the more I think that forbidden question:

— Why?
— Why what?
— Why are you rushing?
— To a meeting.
— To see a friend.
— To meditation.
— That's not what I asked though. I asked you *why*.
— Sorry, I gotta run, I'm late.

Get yourself some SMA, dude. Carpe diem, but slowly.

That's the Way to Travel
by Jan Heller Levi

He was in deep shit is the first line.
The adventurer is writing his 7th novel.
There's a protagonist who uses a wheelchair,

and a murder, and flights of stairs that the protagonist
can't get up or down. Or does he get up and down?
Does he have mysterious powers

that will eventually be revealed?
Few murders have been solved
by a person in a wheelchair.

There was a detective on an old TV series,
but you never saw Ironside stopped outside a door
because his wheelchair was too wide.

It would be good for the reading public
to get to know a character who frequently
can't get into a room, or a store,

or his or her doctor's office. The adventurer's novel
could help change laws, or, at least, attitudes, especially
in the adventurer's native land, where they treat cows

better than cripples. Rimbaud called the bourgeoisie
'the seated.' The adventurer is always seated. And like
the bourgeoisie he acquires lots of possessions. His include:

electric wheelchair, 30-pound battery, battery re-charger,
adapter plug, surge protector, inflatable cushion,
air pump, spare footrests, spare tyres, portable

commode chair, and transfer board. There's also a small,
flexible, plastic-mouthed balloon-like device called a uri-bag.
Lately, the adventurer has been scooting around town,

thinking up ideas for his novel. He gets whomped by sidewalk
potholes, stranded on corners where there isn't a curb-cut,
leapt over and leapt around by pedestrians

who think he's a car. He keeps smiling, so he doesn't
look like one of those bitter cripples. Invariably,
someone passing will nod at him – well, not really at him –

but at his wheelchair, grin and say *That's the way to travel.*
Last night the adventurer and I were talking some non-
bourgeois talk about nomads and gypsies. When

the Europeans tried to destroy Romani culture, they burned
the wheels of the gypsies' wagons. They moved them into concrete
housing projects – running water, electricity. But the gypsies

couldn't stand it. They chopped holes in the roofs so they could
still sleep under the sky. They can cut off our wheels, they said,
but they can't make us choose ceilings over stars.

the crippled

we're among you
always have been
always will

now that you're
getting older
even immortal

one day you too
will be
one of us

look at us now
get to know yourself

Washington Mews & University Pl

I'm Her Wheelchair Man

She looks at me

She looks at me
and says, I love your beautiful wheels

She looks at me,
grabs my wheelchair and rolls away with me

She looks at me
and says, Well, I just knew

She looks at me
and asks, Have you already been hugged eight times?

She looks at me,
bakes gingerbread for me and brings wine too

She looks at me
and says, I'll come to sit at your feet

She looks at me
and races across the room to kiss me on my cheeks

She looks at me,
then calls me very late at night

She looks at me
and stays with me

She looks at me

ALL BODIES ARE DIFFERENT; no two are the same, not even those of 'identical' twins. Not just that: all bodies constantly change, constantly become different. Watch yourself: You're a living *metamorphosis*. You're *living* a metamorphosis.

. . . but because they couldn't understand him, it didn't occur to them, not even to his sister, that he could understand the others . . .
    (F. K.)

BUG STORY

11

Sitting on a bench in the shade of a blooming magnolia in Jefferson Market Garden, a small park in the triangle of Greenwich, W 10th and 6th Ave, Dane observed the soothing spectacle of the awakening beauty of the yellowwoods that dominated the park. He didn't quite remember how he got here and why. It must have been the bucolic peace of the place, its un-New-York-y calm that had lured him here. Indeed, he felt like existing in a bubble, light of thoughts, light of weight, separated from the usual nightmare of the city by no more than a wrought-iron fence. Maybe that was why no one paid attention to him, even though the park was fairly crowded on this warm spring morning. The ants, however, felt unusually, well, antsy. Where they up to something?

For a while Dane relaxed into the soothing spectacle of pedestrians moving past him on the sidewalk outside the garden. Migratory mammals with their programmed destinations. It was good to feel their closeness; it was even better to know that, thanks to the fence between them, they were as removed from him as a parallel world.

Dane gave himself permission to sit back, if only just a bit so as not to hurt his ant skin, and relax. It was true that he killed a substantial number of ants by sitting. But what could he do? He wasn't a horse who stood its entire life.

He called Yess, got the machine, hesitated, then used this medium to ask her what she thought, whether one day he'd evolve into a creature that didn't have to sit any more in order not to hurt his ants. Or even a being that would *hover*? *Fly*, even, as that would be the least ant-killing existence imaginable? He instantly regretted that he'd said that and asked, maybe a bit too abruptly, whether there had been any positive developments in relation to her Assistant Sales Manager position. Not wanting to upset her, he didn't mention what had happened at the Lapin or Gulo Gulo; he'd tell her later, at home, maybe already slightly hovering.

Where did Gale go after leaving him at the Lapin? he wondered. Not to a dentist's office, that much was clear. Dane doubted she'd called Rick to tell him about her former best friend's ants. She was in a quandary: he, Dane, would have been the first person she'd call to talk about such an impossible thing. He blanked. The only image he could conjure was of Gale Force whirling, twister-style, through the sidewalk herds or (more likely) blowing hot puffs of air out of her irritated nose in the back of a cab.

And his boss, Lofty? Invisible but omnipresent as he was, Lofty would be sitting in his tiny office at Gulo like a hungry squid, handling with acumen the day's affairs, forestalling the minutest disturbance in a special evening. Maybe he had already replaced him, with a message on someone's machine that was shorter than the one Dane had just left for Yess. And at 5 p.m., Gulo Gulo would open, and everything would be as it always had been in Lofty's food world.

A part of him understood their reactions. He'd exposed Gale to a shock without any warning; Lofty didn't get much of a heads-up either. They didn't have the opportunity to live with Dane, experience firsthand his being colonized. That had been Yess's privilege. Not to mention the joy of being the one who'd first spotted an ant hatching from his *thing*. He should have prepared them better for the new Dane. He was changing, not Gale or Lofty; he, not the world they were living in. He felt a bit like a product no one wanted. The world, however, was rarely ready for a new product upon first sight; it usually took some getting used to. Dane reminded himself of how long it had taken for, say, farmers' markets to establish themselves. But now they were all the rage. They have so many advantages no one wants to live without any more.

A young mother with her maybe six-year-old son settled down on the bench next to him. It was quite a production to peel the minuscule superhero out of his spandex Spiderman shirt, which looked as tight as a straitjacket. Mom then took off her own lean jacket. When she saw the sweat stains on her blouse, she produced a deep, frustrated sigh. Dane, trying not to stare, found himself pitying her.

He watched a few ants on his shirtsleeve, moving up his arm with unwavering determination. When they reached the platform of his shoulder, they began to circle impatiently; waiting for something?

Behind Dane, there was a low-hanging magnolia branch, its tip almost touching his shoulder. He reached up and pulled the branch down closer. The ants formed a line and, one by one, climbed onto it. There were fifteen of them, among them a queen; it was all they needed for a new bud colony.

The exhausted mom was now struggling with the remains of a melting chocolate bar her superhero son wasn't sure he wanted.

Dane gently released the branch and, with a mixture of pride and worry, watched the first of his children proudly as they disappeared into the tree.

Why don't you switch to my bench? It's cool here, and I'm on my way anyway, Dane said, delightfully stretching his young body and floating away.

FOR A DECADE OR SO, I was two. Walking Me. Rolling Me. I still got as far as a mile or so on my feet. I bought my first wheelchair ahead of time because with one I could get so much further. I've mentioned this. I come back to it because it's hard to understand. People are used to the 'paraplegic narrative': Life Before Accident. Accident. Life After Accident. Simple as that. Of course it's not. In our story-addicted minds, though, it's Plot Point 1 that always occurs exactly 25 per cent into your life. Before that, you live the set-up of your 'normal' life (10 per cent). That's when Opportunity strikes: cool job! sexy mate! treasure buried in a sunken ship! Then, *boom!*, Accident. The rest of your movie is sorting it all out. Miracle surgery (like Batgirl's) would be ideal, but more likely it's Finding Inner Peace (And Finding the Even Sexier Mate) Against All Odds. The SMA narrative is different. I was born with it. My diagnosis was no Plot Point. I both knew already that I had SMA *and* rejected that I had SMA. Here's how it works: 'all voluntary muscles are slowly decreasing in strength over the duration of my life.' There's no Accident. There's no Before, and there's no After. There's only a During. So here we go again. Diagnosis: Life.

IN MY DOPPELGÄNGER YEARS, whether I visited a friend on foot or wheels depended on the nearness of parking spaces and the fitness of my muscles on a given day. Still, it was *something* of a choice. Of course, I sent Walking Me to dates. I remember driving my date home in my car, walking her to her door. On my way back to my car, I collapsed onto the hood, which broke my fall. Maybe she saw it, maybe she didn't. Either way, there was no second date. I was too devastated to call again, and she didn't reach out to me. Come to think of it, I made my major conquests when I chose (or had to be) Rolling Me. Rolling Me may have become the more authentic me. I don't know. Maybe my wheelchair grants me the kind of confidence I couldn't muster on two shaky legs. In my chair, I don't have to worry about my muscle and can focus on being charming. I do know that now it *is* Me. Just Me.

I'M A BIT OBSESSED with these parallel lives of mine. How could I not be? I'm a novelist. I could waddle into a restaurant, throw insults at the owner, then come back in my wheelchair, and the owner wouldn't even recognize me. Fiction! Writing novels is entering the realm of what-ifs, and writing fictional characters is the privilege of living with alter egos. (Obviously, it's also a super-power.) When I published my first novel, many were surprised that it wasn't about my *thing*. (It was a satire about a resourceful writer coming up with a multitude of alter egos in order to advance their career.) I wrote and co-wrote another four novels, three plays and dozens of essays that have nothing to do with my *thing*. Only then did I decide it was time to write the one about my life with a pro-gressive disability. (Actually, it was a Russian writer friend who told me to do it, and it was Jan who encouraged me every step (!) of the way.) I ended it with the first text I wrote for that book, the descrip-tion of a meeting with a Christoph Keller who has Spinal Muscular Atrophy and a Christoph Keller who doesn't have the *thing*.

Washington Pl & 6th Ave

baby born with broken bones into a life of healing bones / hands so strong, fingers so long they play jazz / jazz is sport / jazz is muscle / jazz is weightless / carries you / you carry jazz / mr bill evans: meet mr oscar peterson / hello, mr charles lloyd, come out of hiding / of course, of course, sweet georgia bright / i see you solo / see them carry you across the stage / put you on the piano chair / all fifty dignified pounds all three-two proud feet of you in that beautiful broken body of yours / i know if you move too quickly you'll break a bone / i know you are in pain because you always are / we shits we stare / we able-bodied shits stare, and we disabled shits stare / god, we didn't know you made them *this* ugly / you wiggle yourself into position / oh, please, don't break a bone / but you don't / or maybe you do / and play anyway / twelve notes a chord later we're all beautiful / god is in the room, they said when blind art tatum played / but that isn't true / god is never in the room / mr art tatum was in the room / and now you are in the room / and you say, *ça va?* / and you give us that petruche grin / that most human of grins

for michel petrucciani (1962–1999)

NEW YORK IS the best town for cripples and superheroes.

TODAY I'M GOING OUT to take pictures of the city's dirtiest, most damaged, most crippled curb cuts, pictures of things so ugly that the Dept. of Transportation won't take them as art and will, embarrassed, rush to fix them. But I already decided not to send those pictures either. I don't want the curb cuts repaired any more.

They're the portals to the real New York.

Jump through one of them.

Get stuck in one of them.

Be a supercripple.

Be human.

11th St & University Pl

I WILL BREATHE FOR YOU, Jan said, soon after we met, and I told her how SMA can sometimes lead to respiratory problems, and after the planes hit the World Trade Center she said, I will die with you. What would we have done if we'd been in one of those towers? IN CASE OF EMERGENCY, what are our options? DO NOT USE STAIRS. A sign on each and every elevator in pretty much all of the Western world makes that clear. To me, it spells, in case of emergency, YOU'RE OUT. You and your wife. I would die for Jan. I would force her to leave and hope for my Mike and John. But she wouldn't go. She *is* my Mike and John. No, she's much more than that. Since she can't carry me down a flight of stairs, let alone sixty-eight of them, we'd wait together for our Mike and John. And they'd come. I know they'd come.

Park Avenue South & East 15th St

Kafka wanted to be heavier. I want to be lighter.

Ce n'est pas la colle qui fait le collage, says Max Ernst. *It is not the glue that makes the collage.*

Just once I'd like to get up in the morning and make coffee for Jan while she's still sleeping.

Do you have any idea how many people are jealous of me? They want my car, they want my apartment, they want my art, they want my wife. They want my parking permit. They want my happiness. Yet even though it's one of the secrets of my happiness nobody wants my disability.

You too are the other. All others are blessed with disorder.

All of a sudden something I thought was so wrong was so right.

. . . Art Tatum, with Ben Webster, *All the Things You Are,* the most longing kind of music. You just wait till that sax starts to wail. I long for long walks without wheels, throwing a ball high and far (so the dog has real fun), even running down the stairs and breaking my leg, then impatiently waiting for it to heal . . .

Every cripple is a superhero.

. . . the false ring of the night bell (Kafka), what does it sound like?

I'm learning how *not* to finish things.

The one flaw in *The Metamorphosis*, the most perfect story ever written, is that it is finished.

Write the ending first.

Never write the ending.

Superindex Poem

superafflictions, *42*

superclunky, *16*

supercool, *42*

supercripple, *173*

supercripples, *42*

superhero (cover), *i, iii, 60, 62, 86, 87,*
       101, 131, 154 (4 times),
       166 (twice), *177,*
       180 (twice)

superheroes, *42* (twice), *140, 172*

superhuman, *114*

superindex, *179*

superpower, *42* (twice), *62, 154*

superpowerful, *154*

superpowers, *114* (twice), *154,*
     157

superstar (of rivers), *57*

supervisor, *75, 76* (twice)

ACKNOWLEDGEMENTS

A generous selection from *Every Cripple a Superhero* (including four photographs) has been published in German in Florian Vetsch's translation in Saiten, St Gallen, October 2018, under the title *Jeder Krüppel ein Superheld. Erinnerungssplitter*. An audio version of the playlet on pp. 73–6 has been posted on Saiten's online portal (voices: Julia Kubik and Christoph Keller). 'If My Body': Saiten, 10/2018 (in Clemens Umbricht's German). 'have you noticed?', 'ConEd Poem', 'Where Broadway Bends', 'Cream' in *Gobshite*, 'Summer/Fall 2018' (in English, Spanish, Croatian and German); 'Cream' (in Florian Vetsch's German) in *Poesie Agenda 2019*, Orte Verlag, 2018; 'Where Broadway Bends' in *Quadrant*, January/February 2018; 'The Dane Colony' in *A Worrisome State of Bliss. Manhattan Tales and Other Metamorphosis*, Birutjatjo Press, West Bengal, India, 2016. In August 2020 Limmat Verlag, Zurich, published the German version of this book as *Jeder Krüppel ein Superheld. Splitter aus dem Leben in der Exklusion. The Superhero Complex*, an anthology with texts and artwork inspired by ten texts included in this book will be published by Orte Press, Appenzell, in 2023.

p. 2: *But I say ...* Jan Heller Levi, 'I Lost My Best Friend', *That's the Way to Travel / So sollte man reisen: Selected Poems / Ausgewählte Gedichte* (Pretzien: Moloko Verlag, 2019), p. 42.

p. 21: I reach . . . Muriel Rukeyser, 'St. Roach', in *The Collected Poems of Muriel Rukeyser* (Pittsburgh PA: University of Pittsburgh Press, 2006), p. 533.

p. 23: Time for me . . . Günter Eich, 'Nomaden', in *Gesammelte Werke: Band 1* (Frankfurt: Suhrkamp Verlag, 1991), p. 220. Translated by Christoph Keller.

p. 33: And they felt . . . Franz Kafka, 'The Metamorphosis', in *The Metamorphosis and Other Stories*, translated by Joyce Crick. (Oxford: Oxford University Press, 2009), p. 74.

p. 55: Put on my tie . . . Allen Ginsberg, 'American Sentences', in *Cosmopolitan Greetings: Poems 1986–1992* (New York: Harper Perennial, 1994), p. 107.

p. 57: New York City . . . Peter Malick, 'New York City', from the album *New York City* (Port Washington: eOne / Koch Records, 2003).

p. 63: But I think we need . . . Claudia Rankine, in an interview by Bim Adewunmi and Lynzy Billing, *Buzzfeed*, 27 August 2015.

p. 77: He builds his metamorphoses . . . Elias Canetti, 'Der andere Prozess: Kafkas Briefe an Felice', in *Prozesse: Über Franz Kafka* (München: Carl Hanser Verlag, 2019), p. 281. Translated by Christoph Keller.

p. 85: I'm not here to write, but to be mad. Robert Walser in conversation with Carl Seelig.

p. 85: The way the paths looked . . . Robert Walser, *Der Gehülfe* (Frankfurt: Suhrkamp Verlag, 1985), p. 47. Translated by Christoph Keller.

p. 86: If all else fails . . . Jürg Federspiel, 'Die beste Stadt für Blinde', in *Die beste Stadt für Blinde* (Frankfurt: Suhrkamp Verlag, 1980), p. 28. Translated by Christoph Keller.

p. 99: And yet, the youngest . . . June Jordan, *Soulscript* (Garden City, NY: Zenith Books, 1970), pp. xvii–xviii. Copyright © 1970, 2019 June M. Jordan Literary Estate Trust. Reprinted by permission. www.junejordan.com.

p. 113: Last time I fell . . . Les Murray, 'Vertigo', in *Waiting for the Past* (Collingwood, VIC: BlackInc, 2015), p. 47.

p. 114: These eyes of mine . . . Siamanto (pen name of Atom Yarjanian), 'The Dance', translated by Les Murray, quoted in the epigraph to Les Murray, *Fredy Neptune: A Novel in Verse* (New York: Farrar, Straus and Giroux, 1998), p. xiii.

p. 119: white flight . . . violence to rise . . . scramble to come up with ways . . . Jenny Zhang, 'They Pretend to Be Us While Pretending We Don't Exist', *Buzzfeed*, 11 September 2015.

p. 139: If ever I lose my legs . . . Yusuf Islam / Cat Stevens, 'Moonshadow', from the album *Teaser and the Firecat* (London: Universal Island Records, 1970). Copyright © 1970 Universal Island Records.

p. 142: Everyone comes back . . . Philip Levine, 'Burial Rites', *New Yorker*, 16 April 2007.

p. 156: So it was now . . . Hermann Kinder, *Die böhmischen Schwestern*, (Zurich: Haffmanns Verlag, 1990), pp. 26–7. Translated by Christoph Keller.

p. 158: He was in deep shit . . . Jan Heller Levi, 'That's the Way to Travel', in *Orphan*, by Jan Heller Levi (Farmington ME: Alice James Books, 2014). Copyright © Jan Heller Levi.

p. 163: . . . but because they couldn't understand him . . . Franz Kafka, *Die Verwandlung* (Leipzig: Kurt Wolff Verlag, 1915), p. 31. Translated by Christoph Keller.

p. 177: Ce n'est pas la colle . . . Max Ernst, 'Au-delà de la peinture', in *Max Ernst: Œuvres de 1919 à 1936* (Paris: Cahiers d'Art, 1937), p. 2.

p. 184: I'm happy . . . David Bowie, 'Ashes to Ashes', from the album *Scary Monsters (and Super Creeps)* (New York: RCA Records, 1980).

I'm happy, hope you're happy too.

David Bowie
(1947–2016)